T0209850

# GIRD UP
# THY LOINS
## CALLED FOR IMMEDIATE DUTY

## VIRGINIA HALL

WESTBOW
PRESS*
A DIVISION OF THOMAS NELSON
& ZONDERVAN

WestBow Press books may be ordered through booksellers or by contacting:

WestBow Press
A Division of Thomas Nelson & Zondervan
1663 Liberty Drive
Bloomington, IN 47403
www.westbowpress.com
844-714-3454

Scripture taken from the King James Version of the Bible

ISBN: 978-1-6642-4106-0 (sc)
ISBN: 978-1-6642-4107-7 (hc)
ISBN: 978-1-6642-4105-3 (e)

Library of Congress Control Number: 2021914850

Print information available on the last page.

WestBow Press rev. date: 12/3/2021

# Contents

Chapter 1   THE BREAKING POINT . . . . . . . . . . . . . . . . . . . . . . . 1

Chapter 2   THE CALLING . . . . . . . . . . . . . . . . . . . . . . . . . . . . 15

Chapter 3   BE STILL AND KNOW THAT I AM GOD. . . . . . . . . . . 21

Chapter 4   PREPARING FOR HIS SERVICE . . . . . . . . . . . . . . . . 27

Chapter 5   GREAT FAITH . . . . . . . . . . . . . . . . . . . . . . . . . . . . 35

Chapter 6   IT MUST BE ME. . . . . . . . . . . . . . . . . . . . . . . . . . . 43

Chapter 7   A NEW YEAR . . . . . . . . . . . . . . . . . . . . . . . . . . . . 51

Chapter 8   FLAME OF FIRE . . . . . . . . . . . . . . . . . . . . . . . . . . 55

Chapter 9   IMMEDIATE SURGERY . . . . . . . . . . . . . . . . . . . . . 59

Chapter 10  PEACE, WHERE ARE YOU?. . . . . . . . . . . . . . . . . . 61

Chapter 11  THE CRY OUT . . . . . . . . . . . . . . . . . . . . . . . . . . . 65

Chapter 12  THE BOLD MOVE . . . . . . . . . . . . . . . . . . . . . . . . 71

Chapter 13  WAITING UPON THE LORD . . . . . . . . . . . . . . . . . 87

Chapter 14  THE SMOOTH STONE. . . . . . . . . . . . . . . . . . . . . . 95

Chapter 15  THE DEPARTURE LETTER . . . . . . . . . . . . . . . . . . 99

Chapter 16  MY LAST DAY . . . . . . . . . . . . . . . . . . . . . . . . . . 105

Chapter 17  NEVER EASY . . . . . . . . . . . . . . . . . . . . . . . . . . . 109

## CHAPTER 1

# The Breaking Point

I met Kevin (not his actual name) while deployed in Afghanistan in 2011. I remember it clearly. I was new to the camp and had no idea where any of the latrines were on station. My bladder was full, and I couldn't hold it much longer. I headed to the first two people I saw.

Kevin was standing with another marine, off to the side of the main road, as if they were waiting for someone to pick them up.

I quickly moved closer to them and said, "Can you tell me where the restroom is?"

Kevin shot back the response of a lifetime. He said, "Head that way, then go up the steps, all the way to end, and you'll be there."

I hurried up the stairs and opened the door to find a man urinating in the stall. Startled, he turned and looked at me. I stood there for a brief moment as shock, embarrassment, and frustration rippled through my body. I shook my head, thinking he had sent me to a men's restroom. He must have thought this was a joke. I shut the door and ran back to tell him that his attempt at humor was not appreciated, but by the time I arrived, both men were gone.

Days passed before I saw Kevin again. To be honest, I wasn't even looking for him. I had other important matters to deal with since this was my first experience working as an enlisted aide with absolutely no training in the field. On our next encounter, I gave Kevin a piece of my mind, but the more I explained the situation he'd put me in, the funnier it became. Pretty soon, we were both in the middle of a laughing fit, struggling to catch our breath. I didn't even know his first name yet.

He began talking about a young girl named Emma.

I was so confused. I said, "Who is Emma?"

He said, "Oh, that's our daughter."

If the restroom incident hadn't been enough, now the conversation had become even more awkward. I left, trying to make sense of this man.

As the days passed, thoughts about Emma flooded my mind. Emma is my grandmother's name on my mother's side. If I ever married, I had planned to name my daughter Emma. I remember having a conversation with my mom about that name years before I ever crossed paths with Kevin. Why did he mention "our daughter" in the first place, and what are the odds he'd use the name Emma? My mind kept trying to make sense of it.

To make a long story short, three months later, Kevin and I began doing all the wrong things. Like thousands and thousands of Christian women, I reasoned that I would be the one to lead this man to Christ, thus making our relationship good in God's eyes eventually. Right? Boy, was I wrong! It was because he mentioned the name Emma that I rationalized to myself that Kevin must be the one. It was foolish thinking and did not line up with the Word of God.

How could I lead Kevin to Jesus Christ when I was disobeying His Word from the very beginning? God will not honor sin or deception from His truth. God's Word will never change, not for me or you.

If ye love me, keep my commandments. (John 14:15)

He that hath my commandments, and keepeth them, he it is that loveth me: and he that loveth me shall be loved of my Father, and I will love him, and will manifest myself to him. (John 14:21)

This scripture means that a manifestation of our love for the Lord is *obedience*. My relationship with Kevin was doomed from the very beginning because I was not being obedient to His Word. Despite this, our relationship lasted for a year and a half.

Throughout that time, the Lord was mercifully and compassionately trying to get my attention. I remember hearing clearly, "He will be the destruction of you." These same words were pressed on me two more times during the relationship. I was weak in my walk with the Lord and was unable to let Kevin go because I served the sin in that relationship.

Then the circumstances took a sudden change.

In January 2013, as I was coming out of Bible study, I received an email from Kevin. The message described that he had met someone else. I must have read it a hundred times before the truth finally sank in. By that, I mean *God's truth was revealed in my heart*. It was there, in that church parking lot, where I received a revelation from the Lord. His message was this: I had completely failed in the fear of the Lord.

> The fear of the Lord is the beginning of wisdom: and knowledge of the holy is understanding. (Proverbs 9:10)

> The fear of the Lord is a fountain of life, to depart from the snares of death. (Proverbs 14:27)

> Be not wise in thine own eyes: fear the Lord and depart from evil. (Proverbs 3:7)

I wept for days, repenting of it all. There was one day during this period of repentance when I took seven showers. *Seven showers in one day.* That's how desperately I needed to be cleansed. It was a literal and symbolic cleansing for me; I couldn't get the filth of my sin off with just one shower. I needed seven. Seven signifies completion, perfection. I wept bitterly. My tears were not for Kevin. They were for my Father in heaven. I mourned the way I'd hurt the only One who truly loves me.

> For God so loved the world, that he gave his only begotten Son, that whosoever believeth in him should not perish, but have everlasting life. (John 3:16)

If we would have married, two things are certain: (1) I would have had so much pain in my heart, and (2) I would not have been able to serve God and to fulfill His purpose, plans, and wills for my life. I would have ended up divorced, torn, and broken. In other words, I would not have flourished in my walk with the Lord because Kevin was not the one He had chosen for me.

It didn't end there. There was more I needed to deal with, more purging and cleansing to do within myself—this time deeper in the crevices of my heart. About a week after the breakup email, a coworker became medically disqualified for a deployment. I was next in line, so it was time to start packing. I had one week to prepare for my departure to the most dangerous place in Afghanistan.

If you were to ask me now what the most dangerous place is, I would tell you that it is not Afghanistan or Iraq or any physical *place* at all. The most dangerous place in the world is living without Jesus in your heart. Sealing your heart in Christ allows you to be anywhere in the world with the peace and safety that surpasses all reason or understanding.

I loved serving in the military. I saw beyond myself and would gladly give my own life for this great nation. Having one week to prepare for anything in the military is common. Sometimes you leave the next day. This is the life a soldier, an airman, a marine, and a sailor. It's a worthwhile sacrifice to be a part of something greater.

Two days after my arrival on Leatherneck, I saw Kevin. What were the odds? The chance of a marine and an airman deploying to the same place at the same time twice is exceptionally rare. After that first encounter, I saw him every day with his new girlfriend. A cynic might think that the Lord had sent me there to torment me, but I know that isn't true. God is perfect in His love. The truth is this: even though I had repented and cleansed my life from that relationship, the Lord was dealing with hidden areas of my heart. It was only a matter of time before I would break. Despite my efforts, I had not yet been fully cleansed of my sin because I had not yet let go of it.

By late summer, it finally happened. I hit rock bottom. That evening, while in my quarters, I cried out to God like I had never done before. I was on my knees, facedown, tears flowing uncontrollably.

This wasn't my first deployment. I had been sent to Iraq previously, where mortars were a constant occurrence. Many times you could hear the small-arms firing outside of the camp. There were incidences when the laser interceptors would set off right above me to intercept inbound mortars. I was no stranger to the violence of war. I could deal with the combat attacks, the mortars, and the small-arms firing. But with matters of my heart, I could not bear the pain any longer. Hidden within me was unforgiveness. I had gained the understanding that I had completely failed in the fear of the Lord, but I still had to deal with the unforgiveness in my heart.

> For if ye forgive men their trespasses, your heavenly Father will also forgive you: but if ye forgive not men their trespasses, neither will your Father forgive your trespasses. (Matthew 6:14–15)

The Lord knew that I needed to deal with that immediately. Why else would I have deployed on such a short notice? That night was my breaking point. I wrote down the names of the people I had hurt in my life as well as those who had hurt me. The list must have been three pages long. I tried to reach those I could by phone, and those I couldn't reach, I turned over to Him. Then I burned that list and watched it disappear before my eyes. It was finished! I wrote a letter that evening fully submitting every area of my life to Him, asking Him to fill me with His precious Holy Spirit.

It read:

> Father, in the name of Jesus, I humbly before Your throne today make Jesus Christ the Lord and Master over every area of my life. I make Jesus the Master over where I will live, what kind of work I will do, what will happen to my career, what will happen to my parents, brothers, and sisters, if I will ever get married, and to

whom, if I will have any friends, if I will be successful, if I will ever make any money, what my finances will be, what will happen to my physical body in sickness or health, how God will work in my life, over my home in San Antonio, Texas, over my vehicle, what will happen to my reputation, if I will be popular or not looked up to, what kind of work will I do for the Lord. I will obey God no matter what He asks me to do. I ask You to fill me with Your Precious Holy Spirit right now to enable me to keep the terms of this covenant. I ask You to teach me to hear Your voice, and to teach me from Your Word. I ask You to make further covenants with me as You desire. I thank You for accepting me as Your servant. In the name of Jesus. Amen!

The very next morning, in His infinite grace, I started reading in Psalms. When I read Psalm 2:7–8, the words just lifted off each page.

> I will declare the decree: The Lord hath said unto me, thou art my Son [daughter]; this day have I begotten thee. Ask of me, and I shall give thee the heathen for thine inheritance, and the uttermost parts of the earth for thy possessions. (Psalm 2:7–8)

Again, I wept. Despite my sinful nature with Kevin, His gentle heart called me His daughter. Not even a church had corrected me in this relationship.

Jesus says, "Come unto me, all ye that labor and are heavy laden, and I will give you rest. Take my yoke upon you, and learn of me; for I am meek and lowly in heart: and ye shall find rest unto your souls. For my yoke is easy, and my burden is light."

Jesus didn't come to destroy men's lives; He came to save them. I will never hurt Him like that again. From that point forward, my whole life changed. I was broken within and ready to let the Potter mold the clay. Every breath is His. Everything changed! I had an unexplainable peace within me. It was the peace that surpasses all understanding. It was as though the seed planted within me instantly bloomed into a full tree. Nothing was going to separate us again:

> And the peace of God, which passeth all understanding, shall keep your hearts and mind through Christ Jesus. (Philippians 4:7)

The Lord began manifesting Himself to me in the desert. I was able to see things in the Spirit as He willed and often wondered if anyone else was able to see what I saw. I remember fondly a whirlwind that formed right in front me when there was no breeze in the atmosphere. I only recently have received the revelation from that day.

It is as follows:

My Daughter,

Do you remember the whirlwind from Afghanistan? The one I created from nothing right in front of you. I knew the beautiful skyline would catch your attention once you came out of that building. As you looked at what My hand had created in the sky, I, the Lord, then brought a gentle breeze when there was no breeze. I wanted to show you what I am capable of. The whirlwind I created in front of you grew larger and larger right before your eyes until I made it your height. I saw right to your heart; you were in awe of

My hand. Then I breathed, and the whirlwind passed right through you. You ran to your room and cried out to Me. You asked Me what that was. What did it all that mean? Just like I answered Job by a whirlwind, so I will speak to you by this whirlwind.

The whirlwind is My power and might, but it is also My fury and anger. Like you saw the desert sand taken up from nothing, I also created the sandstorm that covered the camp in darkness shortly thereafter. I knew your thoughts. From the horizon, it looked like a stampede of horses charging for battle in the desert. My hand is in all things. Nothing is hidden from Me. Even though you stepped out of your room to see inside the storm, I kept you safe from harm. I protected you and will always be with you. I will never leave you, Daughter. You are mine. I have redeemed you.

My conversations with the Lord were quite interesting after all this. I remember one time, in humor, I specifically asked the Lord, "How many hairs do I have on my head?"

Later, I repented for it, expressing to Him, "You don't have to tell me; I know You know all things, Lord."

Being liberated by Jesus and filled with His precious Holy Spirit, I had to settle the most important thing in my heart with Him. I never want to hurt Him like I did when I was with Kevin. I wanted to serve Him acceptably. He knew what I was about to ask.

I asked. "Lord, if Jesus's delight was in the fear of the Lord, shouldn't that be my delight? Father, let that be my delight, Father, for quick understanding that I may serve You acceptably all the days of my life. I don't want to hurt You as I did before. I know I am not perfect, but You are Lord. You are a perfect Father. Keep me centered on the fear of the Lord. Amen!"

It was like I was at attention, and He gave the commands.

Still deployed, I came across a ministry, led by a woman and based in the United States, that shared a beautiful love letter from the Lord on their website. I eventually went to work for this ministry (more on that later). I had only read just a few sentences when my spirit began to leap for joy. Because of this joy, I decided to print the letter so I could read it slowly and carefully.

Those of us who have deployed to the desert understand the difficult environments we had to bear. The military provides Morale, Welfare, and Recreation (MWR) tents, common areas to help us relax and enjoy a good movie at times. This is where I had to go to print the love letter. As I made my way to the MWR tent, I was unaware that a mighty occurrence was about to unfold.

I arrived without incident, but before I even printed that letter, the tent shook like as though an explosion had occurred. The items inside rattled and shifted on the shelving. There was just one other individual in the tent with me at the time, and we ran outside to engage in battle. We were ready. However, when we stepped outside, we looked in every direction, only to find there was no explosion. No mushroom cloud in sight. *Absolutely no evidence of an attack.* We looked at each other in confusion.

As we walked back inside, the Lord had my full attention. He was about to deliver a letter that would touch my heart and lead me into a deeper understanding of Himself. It was anointed and wonderfully written. It spoke right to my heart. I wept.

To thank that ministry for their service, I decided to mail them a simple thank-you card. I remember the card had a stunning red cardinal on its front cover, and the cost was free. To be honest, it was all I had. About two months later, I receive a letter enclosed with one of the ministry leader's books. I didn't think I would get a response to my card, so this was a pleasant surprise. In the letter, she requested my contact information so we could schedule a visit once I returned home.

At the time, I was surprised at how close I was stationed. I was excited about the proximity. Since I was born-again and filled with the Spirit in Afghanistan, I surrounded myself with women who served and loved the Lord with all their hearts while there. Ironically enough, they weren't Americans. I would often meet them at their quarters even though it was off-limits for Americans to visit. I was thirsty for Christ and wanted to be surrounded by people who loved Him diligently. I saw their hearts and yearned for their fellowship.

These women had a genuine love for Christ that I had not seen in any American on that camp—not even the ones who attended church. One night, while in a friend's quarters, my friend from Kenya (who worked as a contractor on the camp) made a bold statement. She had prophesied to me that I was going to work at this ministry. Not thinking any of this, as soon as I returned home, I set a date and time to meet with the ministry leaders in person. We met at a Red Lobster, and our conversation was delightful. After our meal, we went our separate ways. A few weeks later, they asked to meet again for lunch. This time, I had to drive to Conway, Arkansas. The conversation went well again. Deep down, I knew both encounters were a test. My heart was being evaluated by them. After another great lunch, we again went our separate ways.

On their drive home, they called me and asked if I would work for them. They told me they believed the Holy Spirit had confirmed this to them. I explained I still had two years left on my military contract to fulfill. I couldn't just leave the military because I wanted to. They insisted that I come to visit the ministry soon. So, I agreed to the visit.

When I arrived, the minute I stepped through the main office door, I sensed in my spirit that I was to work for them. So, without hesitation, I said yes. It was settled that day. I would be a part of this ministry once I retired from the United States Air Force.

I continued to serve faithfully in the military, knowing now where I would go once finished.

Something happened to me the day I saw those two towers fall on September 11, 2001. Most of us can remember that day to the exact detail. Those of us who have served in the military understand obedience. We understand obeying the orders given to us. It's instilled into our very being in basic training: the knowledge of hierarchy and the importance of obedience. We remain faithful and true until the very end, sacrificing our own lives for something greater than ourselves. Because of this, I began to seek the Lord diligently on my journey after the military. I needed confirmation that I was making the right decision. So, I sought the Lord day and night.

Do you remember when I asked the Lord how many hairs do I have on my head? Six months later, he answered me. The Lord tends to speak to us in the most awkward moments of our lives. The places where you least expect it are often where the Lord reveals Himself. One day at work, while in the restroom of all places, the Lord revealed to me the number of hairs on my head. There was a number that had captured my attention on my pant trouser because it was handwritten. I took a closer look. As I did this, instantly I heard, "Those are the number of hairs on your head."

My spirit leaped within me. I was filled with joy and in awe of Him! I ran to the first person I saw and told her what just had happened. She wasn't as excited as I was. But I had to share what had just been revealed to me. As the days went by, the Lord kept manifesting Himself to me. I became so thirsty for His Living Word that I had to enroll into a school of ministry to gain as much knowledge as I could about God's kingdom. It was at this school that the Lord revealed the calling in my life. I had asked, and He had answered. I wanted all these things added unto me as His Word declares:

> But seek ye first the kingdom of God, and his righteousness; and all these things shall be added unto you. (Matthew 6:33)

CHAPTER 2

# The Calling

——

I lived in base quarters, which means home was but a short distance from work. Every day, I would go home for lunch to let my dog outside. This day was no different. At the end of my workday, as soon as I arrived home, I grabbed my Bible from the dining table, sat outside with my dog, and began reading 2 Timothy. When I arrived at chapter 4, I noticed a breeze had come in. The more I read, the stronger the breeze became. Finally, the breeze was so intense that I looked up to observe my surroundings. I saw the branches of the trees swaying as if they were bowing down to Him.

Suddenly, I heard what sounded like a stadium of people clapping. It was so profound! I stood to my feet, closed my eyes, and just listened. It was as if I was surrounded by thousands upon thousands of the Lord's angels in this stadium, and they were all cheering for me and clapping for me. Nothing like that had ever happened to me before.

> For ye shall go out with joy, and be led forth with peace: the mountains and the hills shall break forth before you into singing, and all the trees of the field shall clap their hands. (Isaiah 55:12)

I must have stood there for a minute. It was one of the most remarkable things I have ever heard in my life. With my eyes closed, I said to the Lord, "Surely, this can't be for me."

Thinking nothing more of the situation, I went inside, changed my clothes, and headed to the store. On my return home, I was pulled over by the military base police in which the officer accused me of disobeying the "when blinking" 15 MPH speed limit sign. I was traveling at 30 MPH.

I asked the officer to forgive me for speeding and then politely relayed to him that the lights were not blinking. He took my identification and walked back to his vehicle to write the ticket. Minutes later, he returned, handed me my driver's license, and said, "Here you go."

As he walked away, I asked, "Where's my ticket?"

He replied, "You are good, ma'am."

I thanked the Lord all the way home.

In my short walk with the Lord thus far, I had realized that how you handle a situation will determine its outcome. Do I revile in return or defend myself in this case even though I knew I had done nothing wrong? Or in all my circumstances, do I give it to the Lord—no matter what, even when falsely accused—or do I handle my way like all the other times I did when I did not have Christ in my heart? I can tell you stories of those days. But I want to focus on the goodness of our Lord and Father, Jesus Christ. He is able!

Who, when he was reviled, reviled not again; when he suffered, he threatened not; but committed himself to him that judgeth righteously? (1 Peter 2:23)

Dearly beloved, avenge not yourselves, but rather give place unto wrath: for it is written Vengeance is mine; I will repay, saith the Lord. (Romans 12:19)

When I arrived home, I hurried in to let my dog outside again. While standing outside, I noticed there was no breeze. So, I asked, "Lord, where is the breeze?"

A sweet, soft, gentle voice said, "Do you remember what you were reading when I brought the breeze?"

I looked around to see if anyone was near, and then I responded, "Yes, Lord, I do."

"Go read it again," He declared.

I ran back inside, grabbed my Bible, went back outside, and read 2 Timothy 4 again. Thinking He might bring the breeze again, I read it as carefully as if He was reading it to me. It read:

I charge thee therefore before God, and the Lord Jesus Christ, who shall judge the quick and the dead at his appearing and his kingdom; Preach the word; be instant in season, out of season; reprove, rebuke, exhort with all long suffering and doctrine. For the time will come when they will not endure sound doctrine; but after their own lusts shall they heap to themselves teachers, having itching ears; and they shall turn away their ears from the truth, and shall *be turned* unto fables. (2 Timothy 4:4)

When I arrived at verse 5, my spirit leaped yet again. It was as if the words lifted off the page:

> But watch thou in all things, endure afflictions, do the
> work of an evangelist, make full proof of thy ministry.
> (2 Timothy 4:5)

Then I asked the Lord, "Have you called me to be an evangelist? Am I an evangelist, Lord? If this is what I am to become, I will do as you say. This charge is no insignificant matter before You and Your Son, Jesus Christ. I will need You more than ever!" My thoughts quickly shifted, and I considered Saul's initial response before he was to become king:

> Am not I a Benjamite, of the smallest of the tribes of
> Israel? And my family the least of all the families of
> the tribe of Benjamin? Wherefore then speakest thou
> so to me? (1 Samuel 9:21)

My reaction was similar. With my heart's initial response to the breeze, I didn't believe any of this could possibly be for me. Who am I? I have done nothing worthy for Him. I am nothing. Samuel said he will tell Saul all that is in his heart. I strongly believe Saul already knew what was in his heart. I knew what was in my heart. I just didn't believe that He would want to use me. My thought life needed a lot of work back then, and I am still growing in spiritual maturity toward the Lord. I will forever be learning. God's goodness will always lead you to Him. He means what He says when He says it.

Just like all the writings this the book, I hope it draws you, the reader, to Jesus Christ. That is my prayer. That these testimonies pull you closer to His heart. The Lord is good, and He does what is good. His judgments are righteous. I have come a long way in understanding His goodness. I rest on the things He has done for me. He is a companion to all those who fear Him. The secrets of the Lord are with those who fear Him. Deep inside my heart, I have such a desire for the lost, those who are captive, and those who know not of His goodness.

CHAPTER 3

# Be Still and Know that I Am God

———

In 2015, I was given orders to a remote island in the middle of the ocean. Even though I had the desire to work for the ministry, I still had to fulfill my military obligations. I loved serving in this capacity—putting others before myself—that is a military lifestyle. It was a core value: service before self. I had no idea I was about to spend a year in one of the most beautiful places I had ever seen. It was there that I became still, knowing that He is God. There was nowhere for anyone to go, no shopping malls, no grocery store (a convenience store only), no toilet paper (a month without), no kids, no pets, no cell phones (for me anyway), no visiting another city or loved ones, just thirty-seven miles of untouched natural beaches to sit on, read, and spend time with the Lord. I witnessed the most wonderful sunrises and sunsets here. They were breathtaking moments.

Even when the storms raged on the island, I saw the hand of God on my life as I ventured into them. Just like I did in the sandstorm in Afghanistan, I often stepped out into the tropical storms on the island. I knew the Lord would shield me. There were many times I would let my feet sink into the soft warm sand, expressing unto the Lord:

> How precious also are thy thoughts unto me, O God!
> How great is the sum of them! If I should count them,
> they are more in number than the sand: when I awake,
> I am still with thee. (Psalm 139:17–19)

The beach extended for miles, and I could see the grains of sands as far as the east is to the west. His thoughts for me are so many; there was no way I could count them. So are His thoughts for you. Who can count them?

While stationed on the island, I applied for retirement. However, my request was rejected twice. The justification received from headquarters was they would not allow me to retire while serving overseas. I had no choice but to wait upon my return to the States to apply for retirement. I had not told any of my leadership at that point that I planned to retire. Now that everyone knew, they often would ask, "Are you sure?"

I relayed my plans and how I had a position at an international ministry available for me. Have you ever been told you were making the biggest mistake of your life? I sought the Lord diligently on this critical decision. This isn't something I took lightly, yet support was in short supply.

I believe there are three major decisions a person will make in their lifetime. The first one is the most important: accepting Jesus as

Lord and Savior! Honestly, I can stop right there because He is all we need. But there are two others.

The second is what career you will have. In other words, to what purpose or mission will you devote your God-given talents and energy? For me, comfort and convenience were never factored into my career decisions. Frankly, if you're looking for comfort or convenience, the military is probably the last option you should choose. It's a sacrifice! But having a profession that gives you a sense of purpose, an opportunity to serve that which is bigger than the self, makes all the difference. I enjoyed every bit of my military career. That doesn't mean every moment was good; there were challenges and hard days as well. Through both, I was refined and molded into a leader who genuinely loves those in my charge. I stayed focused on the big picture; it outweighed everything.

It's the same when it comes to our relationship with Jesus; success requires us to focus on the eternal perspective. The eternal perspective outweighs current circumstances.

The third critical decision one will make in their lifetime is who you will marry. This is no small matter before the Lord. He created marriage. Like I stated before, I had reasoned to myself that Kevin was the one for me. *I* tried to birth this marriage; God didn't. We all know what happens when we do something outside of God's Word.

God won't honor lies, but he does offer grace and redemption. When making these three major decisions about your life, remember that making the first decision—accepting Jesus Christ as your Lord and Savior—will arm you to make the other two decisions with a sense of direction and purpose. If you listen to Him, you will know which career and which spouse are right for you. The hardest part for all of us is having the patience to wait for the perfect plan He has in store for our lives. So often, as Christians, we try to rush or write the story. In doing so, we hijack our own lives instead of letting God guide us in these vital choices.

I loved being on the island. It was a time to be still and know that He is God. Because of the comments I received, I sought the Lord deeper about retiring from the Air Force. The opinions of my colleagues began to influence my decision. Was I making the right choice? Not once was there a question in my spirit. When it came to this choice, I experienced a feeling of peaceful purpose every time I prayed about it.

One day, while praying in spirit and truth, the voice of the Lord said, "I will bless your military career; you will go all the way. But if you choose the ministry (service), I will show you more of my heart."

I wept. In that very moment, I received my confirmation from the Lord. I knew I wanted more of His heart. I thirsted to be closer to Him. I began asking Him to prepare me for His service. How was I to serve Him? I cried out, "Teach me, Father, through Your Word. I will obey. I want to know Your heart is my greatest desire."

After receiving this confirmation, it didn't matter what anyone said to me about retiring. It was settled.

Since I was on the most beautiful island in the world, I took full advantage. The fishing was amazing, the waters were crystal clear, and the local village church was a joy to be a part of. I met some of the most loving people at that church. It was the first time I sang in a choir. What a joy it was to sing unto the Lord. My heart rejoiced in the opportunity to worship that way.

One night in June, I received an urgent prayer request from a cousin. She asked how I was doing and said, "I know you are a woman of faith, and I humbly ask for your prayers for my five-month-old daughter. She will be undergoing a bone marrow biopsy on Thursday. Doctors want to know what exactly she has because other tests have failed to diagnose why she has low neutrophil cell counts."

Without hesitation, I immediately went before the Lord in prayer. I prayed for a miracle. Afterward, I sensed I should text her the prayer so that she would stand in agreement with it: "It is by faith we receive healing, comfort, provision, and direction. There is no other way. In our hearts, we believe it is done."

She quickly replied, "Thank you." She had read the prayer out loud while holding her daughter and believing in faith that her baby was healed. She was filled with gratitude.

As the doctor's appointment drew near, I continued to intercede for her daughter daily. Throughout the New Testament, Jesus performed miracles and healed the sick. His words after He would pray have always caught my attention:

> And he said unto her, daughter, thy faith hath made thee whole. (Mark 5:34)

> Stand up and go; your faith has made you well. (Luke 17:19)

The two blind men followed Jesus and said:

> Thou son of David, have mercy on us. And when he was come into the house, the blind men came to him: and Jesus saith unto them, believe ye that I am able to do this? They said unto Him, Yea, Lord. Then touched he their eyes, saying, according to your faith be it unto you. (Matthew 9:27–29)

I believe in my cousin's response to me, "believing in faith she will be healed," the Lord extended His everlasting arm and healed her daughter with a miracle. He healed the child instantly. The evidence of that came days later when the doctors were not able to find anything wrong with her. Everything came back normal. He healed her because her faith made her well. My cousin contacted me with the good news, and I told her that we needed to praise Jesus. And we did just that. Praise God!

My faith increased. One night, while I was sound asleep, I woke up at about three o'clock and saw something standing at the foot of my bed. It was a dark shadow of a tall, midsized man. I could not see anything but his silhouette. I was frightened, but I was also very tired. I rubbed my eyes to get a clear view, but I still saw only a shadow. I said, "I'll deal with you in the morning." Then I fell right back asleep. Once I woke up, I immediately dealt with it in the only effective way: through prayer. Nothing like that ever happened to me again while on the island.

CHAPTER 4

# Preparing for
# His Service

---

After the island, I reported to a base in Northern California. Before my arrival, I informed my superintendent of my decision to retire. Even though I was retiring, I still performed my duties with excellence. Nothing changed from that aspect:

> And whatsoever ye do, do it heartily, as to the Lord,
> and not unto men. (Colossians 3:23)

While stationed in California, the Lord was about to teach me another facet of His personality. One Sunday afternoon, my day started normal. I had a full day planned with my good friend Naomi. We were going to have lunch followed by mini-golf to improve our short game. Our lunch was delicious, but while we were at the mini-golf course, the unexpected occurred. I received a call from one of my subordinates.

He said there was an emergency; a disaster was about to happen. He had just heard on the news that the Oroville Dam in Oroville, California, was about to break. This was the first time I had even heard of the dam crisis.

He asked, "What do we do?"

Ten thousand thoughts flowed through my mind. I told him to stand by. I needed confirmation. Naomi and I began calling our superiors to confirm what was going on. She received the notification first.

Immediately, we began contacting all our subordinates to leave their homes quickly and head to higher ground—all the while keeping them calm. Despite the urgency of the situation, we found it effortless to do so. They all had families, and there was no time to waste. Most of us lived in the break path of the dam. We had become evacuees! If the dam broke, it was estimated we would have five to fifteen minutes to get out.

I had seven subordinates I served as the director of logistics for my unit, and I was responsible for each one of them. Their safety of and the safety of their families became my priority. All obeyed my orders and reported back to me every hour with their sitrep (a periodic report of the current military situation). I needed confirmation they were all safe. I was also accountable to report up to my superior.

In the midst of all this, I had to take care of myself as well. Knowing everyone under me was heading to safety gave me peace. Within an hour, things had shifted in our lives. There was no way I would leave my dog behind.

Naomi and I quickly headed home. On our drive, we devised our escape as well. She convinced me she would pick me up and drive us to Sacramento for safety. That was our glorious plan. Our leaders told us to get to safety as well, and we did exactly what we were told. I quickly prepared my home for the flood while rebuking fear and the breakage. I prayed for protection. Finally, I packed supplies, a bag for my dog, and a small bag for me. At approximately seven o'clock, we were heading south to a major city—just like everyone else. Little did I know God had other plans for us.

Stuck in traffic, while sitting in Naomi's jeep, I heard the audible voice of the Lord again. This time, He wasn't so sweet and soft like He was when He brought the breeze to reveal my calling. He was firm. He said, "What are you doing? I did not teach you to run."

Without hesitation, I turned to Naomi and asked, "How would you feel about turning around and heading to base?" We knew we could be airlifted to safety. We served in the world's greatest military. Anything was possible. She immediately agreed, and we turned around. We were the only ones heading in the wrong direction—going against the grain. In an effort not to make Naomi uncomfortable, I quietly prayed for His everlasting strength and courage against the unknown. A boldness had come over me; that peace surpassed all understanding that confirmed to me no harm would come to us.

On our way to the base, we stopped for gas. Only premium gas was available at the pump. There was no attendant in sight, and everything was securely locked. The gas line was very long. Some people were in panic mode, and some were not. I saw the fear in their faces as they waited their turn.

When it was our turn, the news media began interviewing Naomi. I, on the other hand, continued to fill the tank with gas.

The woman at the gas pump in front of us only had cash. Since there wasn't an attendant and the doors to the station were locked, she kindly asked if I would buy her gas with my card. She offered the cash in return. I looked at her and then looked inside her vehicle and saw her children. I wasn't going to be responsible for this woman if anything were to happen to her because I didn't give pay for her gas. Forty dollars to potentially save a life is an easy decision. Jesus had paid the price for this family whether she knew it or not:

> For God so loved the world, that he gave his only
> begotten Son, that whosoever believeth in him should
> not perish, but have everlasting life. (John 3:16)

I pumped her tank full of gas, and then we proceeded to the base. Throughout the evening and into the early morning hours, we were busy preparing the base for evacuees. Naomi and I heard from someone that volunteers were needed to drive into the dangerous spillway to gather people in hospitals, including nurses. Hours after this need was expressed, no one had volunteered to go.

At three o'clock in the morning, I sensed I was to go collect these people and bring them to safety. But there was no way I could go by myself; nobody would let that happen. I needed someone to go with me.

Naomi and I began discussing the task, the risks, and the logistics. Finally, I said, "Do you trust me? I believe no harm will come to us." Resting on what I previously received from the Lord, I believed it to be true. I rested on His promise.

She finally agreed to go. She briefed her leadership on our plans, and they approved it on the spot. The plan was straightforward even though the dam could break at any time. We picked up a bread truck (a flight line vehicle that transported people to and from the locations on the flight line), grabbed a radio (code name: Cowgirl), and headed into the spillway. My dog was by our side the whole time.

After we gathered all the patients and nurses who could fit into the truck, we headed straight to base. Naomi, with her gentle heart, still obeyed those traffic signals. It's instilled into us to do the right thing. Deep down inside each of us, we know what's right and wrong. I'm guilty of making the wrong decisions when it comes to "small" situations like this, but not Naomi.

One particular red light that Naomi stopped at was the longest red light I've ever sat through in my life. I looked at her and thought, *What are you doing? Why are we stopping at red lights?* She had taken on this task with trust in me, so I didn't say a word. Whatever was on her mind at that time, I couldn't tell you. Here's what I can say: when we are faced with uncertain circumstances, when we are in the midst of the storm, that is where you will begin to see the manifestations of a true leader.

That night, Naomi stood out as one of those leaders. I saw it in her. Her heart enlarged. She put others above her own life. She trusted me enough to venture out into the unknown, placing her own life in danger as well. Faith in the Lord carried me. Had I not heard Him speak in the beginning, while on our way to Sacramento, I would have followed suit with the rest of the evacuees who were heading to safety. In that moment, I had so much respect for her because of the selfless attitude in her heart that brought forth boldness in her actions.

> Greater love hath no man than this, that a man lay
> down his life for his friend. (John 15:13)

When the light finally turned green, Naomi, deep in thought, remained still.

I finally said, "Naomi, it's green." I wasn't mean or angry at her for stopping at the light. I knew in my heart no harm would come to us while in the path of the spillway. I had peace. Glory to God!

We made it out of the danger zone safely. To this day, there is no doubt in my mind that the Lord's angel protected us every step of the way and prevented that dam from breaking. He knew we would be in its spillway.

> For he shall give his angels charge over thee, to keep thee in all thy ways. They shall bear thee up in their hands, lest thou dash thy foot against a stone … Because he hath set his love upon me, therefore will I deliver him: I will set him on high, because he hath known my name. He shall call upon me, and I will answer him: I will be with him in trouble; I will deliver him, and honour him. With long life will I satisfy him, and shew him my salvation. (Psalm 91:11–12, 14–15)

> For it is written, He shall give his angels charge over thee, to keep thee. And in their hands they shall bear thee up, lest any time thou dash thy foot against a stone. (Luke 4:10–11)

This wasn't just for Naomi or me. Many others cried out that night to the Lord, and those prayers were answered. He protected us during this perilous time.

That night, because we trusted God in all things, He provided us the peace, strength, and courage needed to provide reception for more than three hundred evacuees, to rescue twenty-five ambulatory patients from the spillway, to arrange shelter in the base gym (including sleeping bags), and to provide food delivery for evacuees. We led the airmen with direction, orders, and instructions of duty to fulfill one mission; save lives. Naomi's selfless attitude glowed all night. Everything flowed that night for us. It was in good order! Praise God!

While stationed in California, it was hard to find a church home. I must have searched for months before I finally found one that settled in my spirit. I drove forty-five minutes to and from church every Saturday to attend their service. It was worth the drive.

In May, while attending a Christian conference at my church with my younger sister, Faith, the atmosphere was filled with the Lord's presence. When I say that, I mean He came in like a mighty wind. One of the sessions at the conference was on the gifts of the Holy Spirit. It was a wonderful lesson that truly inspired me to pursue the gifts.

Every word spoken that day reached my heart. On that day, I was delivered from a major stronghold in my life. Nobody laid hands on me. No one prayed over me. Praise God! I was set free. For more than a year, I had prayed and counterattacked my sinful nature proclaiming God's promises and Word over my life. I often replaced my own sinful thoughts with James 4:7. It worked! Changing my thought life was key to my transformation. I learned to replace negative thoughts with the truth. I practiced making every thought obedient unto the Lord Jesus Christ. I needed His Word in me to guard my thoughts and my heart because it is eternal.

> Heaven and earth shall pass away, but my words shall not pass away. (Matthew 24:35)

> Submit yourselves therefore to God. Resist the devil, and he will flee from you. (James 4:7)

> Casting down imaginations, and every high thing
> that exalteth itself against the knowledge of God, and
> bringing into captivity every thought to the obedience
> of Christ. (2 Corinthians 10:5)

Immediately after I was set free, Isaiah 58:12 flashed through my mind. I had no idea what it said. On the drive home from the conference, I had my sister look it up:

> And they that shall be of thee shall build the old waste
> places: thou shalt raise up the foundations of many
> generations; and thou shalt be called, the repairer of the
> breach, the restorer of paths to dwell in. (Isaiah 58:12)

My spirit leaped again when I heard the words *build, raise, repairer,* and *restorer.* I accepted this from the Lord, thanking Him all the way home.

Two days later, before I even stepped out of bed, I heard these words: "Wield the gifts."

Of course, with my fine education, I should have known what *wield* meant. I'll be the first person to admit *I didn't.* I don't claim to know all things. The more I grow in my spiritual maturity, the more I feel like I'm starting over. I can't tell you how many times I feel like I've started over in my Christian walk. Not knowing the definition of *wield* confirmed to me it wasn't my thought.

Wield means "to have and to use with full command or power; to manage as to wield a sword; to wield the scepter." When we are filled with the Holy Spirit, we have all the gifts available to us as born-again Christians. I was being told to stir them up. So, I pressed into the Lord for discernment, wisdom, and a deeper understanding so that I could boldly move as He purposed and willed.

## CHAPTER 5

# Great Faith

—

Trusting in the Lord with what was given to me about revealing more of His heart, I stepped out in faith, wholeheartedly resting on that one word. It's all I had.

The day had finally come when it was time to say goodbye to my military career, having served faithfully and honorably. Just like the centurion in Luke 7:6–9, who understood his role having a servant heart in leadership, obedient and submitted to the leader appointed over them. Yet having the soldier's best interest in mind to care, protect, nurture, shape, and mold them into leaders themselves.

> And when he was now not far from the house, the centurion send friends to him, saying unto him, Lord, trouble not thyself: for I am not worthy that thou

shouldest enter under my roof: Wherefore neither thought I myself worthy to come unto thee: but say in a word, and my servant shall be healed. For I also am a man set under authority, having under me soldiers, and I say unto one, Go, and he goeth; and to another Come, and he cometh; and to my servant, Do this, and he doeth it. When Jesus heard these things, he marveled at him, and turned to him about, and said unto the people that followed him, I say unto you, I have not found so great faith, no, not in Israel. (Luke 7:6–9)

With more than ninety days of accumulated leave, I was released from my unit in July with an effective retirement date in October. Before that date came, I quickly began working for the international ministry before the end of summer; after all these years of waiting, the day finally arrived. Unlike my initial response when I first visited the ministry, from the moment I arrived, I sensed things were out of order.

I want you to know my heart before you proceed to the next chapters of this book. It is not my intention to destroy any ministry. That's not my heart. The Lord promised He would show me more of His heart. It is my prayer that these words encourage you in your walk with the Lord, and that in the storms, you will pursue Him first in all things, especially as we move into these end-times. He is first in every area of our hearts. He desires repentance. He desires His children to seek Him diligently in every area of our lives. Please remember those were my actions as you continue to read.

I sought Him in all things before I moved in any direction— just like I did when I made the bold decision to retire. I will not do anything unless I receive direction from Him. Even if it is just one word or no words, it is clear. I didn't respond out of emotion or became reactive in situations. I pressed deeper into the Lord Jesus Christ's wisdom, understanding, and discernment. I was new to His ministry, and I was eager to be taught by Him. I wanted to do what He had called me to do at this ministry. I knew God had sent me for something more than what I could see immediately.

The home that had been prepared for me was not so prepared to live in. It was filthy, infested with insects, smelled of rat urine, and there was water in the air-conditioning vents, which only added to the terrible smell. The temperature inside must have been at least ninety degrees. It was unbearable, and no one in their right mind would have stayed there. I checked into a hotel that was about eleven miles away. For the first two weeks at this ministry, I contemplated leaving. The condition of the home was a red flag to me, and I saw it as a reflection of the leadership. But since I had received conviction from the Lord, I stayed and remained obedient to Him. Just from seeing my home alone, I knew much would be needed to rebuild and restore this ministry. My life in the military, while *deployed*, provided better conditions of living than this ministry provided.

I cried out to the Lord day by day. *What is this? What's going on?* I received no response. I had pictured a ministry that was full of joy, peace, love, and righteousness. Everything turned out to be the opposite. Lesson number one in the Lord's service—what I imagined about His service—was irrelevant. Most people would probably have left that first day, but I knew this wasn't about me. It wasn't about the living conditions. It wasn't about any tangible thing. This was about the matters of His heart. God had a purpose for me here, and I wanted to see it through. It was about His purpose, will, and plans.

That was my heart's burning desire: to follow his direction and be a tool for His purpose.

My first night in the home, as I prepared the bed, I flipped the mattress in the master bedroom. A brown recluse spider crawled out of one of the small metal crevices on the side of the mattress. There was absolutely no way I could sleep on that. I don't know how to explain it, to be honest. I've seen some worn and torn mattresses in my military career, but I just couldn't sleep on that one—not after that spider. So, I slept on the floor. The very next day, with permission, the mattress was replaced with a fresh one. Out with the old, in with the new! This was the way I was going to approach things. I was going to repair, rebuild, and restore where they allowed me.

In all the renovations I wanted to do, I asked permission first. I made sure I received approval before proceeding forward. In all my requests, I received a quick yes—do whatever you want! And I did just that. I started to have a set routine as the days passed. I didn't care what the task was; I knew this was where I was supposed to be, even with the conditions the home. My eyes were set on the eternal perspective. My heart desired to serve the Lord in any possible way. If this was it, then this was it. I was eager to learn and be taught in the things of the Lord. However, He wanted to do that, I had a willing heart. I remained moldable.

In the military, we often received feedback on comprehensive assessments to evaluate our work performance. I wasn't sure if this was the same in ministry. This was all new to me, and I wanted to be pleasing in the sight of the Lord. So, I spoke first. I told Sarah I would do all they asked, like Joseph at Potiphar's home:

> And the Lord was with Joseph, and he was a
> prosperous man; and he was in the house of his master

the Egyptian. And his master saw that the Lord was with him, and that the Lord made all that he did to prosper in his hand. And Joseph found grace in his sight, and he made him overseer over his house, and all that he had put into his hand ... And he left all that he had in Joseph's hand. (Genesis 39:2–4, 6)

Whatever needed to be done—large, small, difficult, or easy—I did it with a cheerful heart. I never complained or murmured. That was not in my nature to do, and I know this type of behavior is not in God's nature as well. There are many lessons I learned while serving in the military. After I saw those two towers fall on September 11, 2001, something happened deep within me. It was too close to home, and I wanted to be used in any capacity possible to protect this great nation, even if it meant giving my life. I was determined to make the best of any situation, no matter where the military sent me.

I was determined to make the best of any situation no matter where He sent me. My attitude was to serve Him acceptably:

With good will doing service, as to the Lord, and not to men: Knowing that whatsoever good thing any man doeth, the same shall he receive of the Lord, whether he be bond or free. (Ephesians 6:7–8)

My hours were great. I reported at seven o'clock and worked until two. I often arrived early to feed the animals, and then I reported to the main office to prepare all the orders. There were quite a few orders dated from months past; one was dated almost a year prior. It took several days to fulfill all the back orders. Unlike the military, there was absolutely no stress working for this ministry. The process was very simple, but everything, including books in the stockroom, was not properly stored. Items were all over the place, which made it difficult to find products to fulfill orders. The very first mission they gave me was to create an inventory-tracking system for quick reference followed by organizing the books in the stockroom by author.

This took more than a month, but I did my best with what they gave me to use. The stockroom became an efficient workplace to get orders in and out in a sufficient amount of time. It wasn't hard to streamline the process with both the stockroom and the tracking system. We now could view what was in stock and what needed to be back-ordered.

During the evenings, I spent my time repairing the home. I ripped out all the carpet, laid vinyl wooden flooring, painted the walls, and cleaned like I had never cleaned before. I was determined to make it a livable place. It took at least a month to complete. I devoted most of my time in the evenings to cleaning. Nevertheless, I continued to serve the ministry faithfully.

When I first arrived, Sam saw my shadow box. A shadow box is a military tradition one receives as a gift upon retirement. It summarizes a servicemember's faithful works of service, describing all the accomplishments achieved in one box. My shadow box was simple. Everything that ever meant anything to me when I served was placed into my box. The most important item in the box was the letter I wrote to the Lord when I was born-again in the desert.

Sam and I had our military backgrounds in common. He mentioned he had served as a colonel. He said he was a Vietnam pilot who was shot down in combat. He had such a remarkable military career, judging from all the stories he told. I was surprised he didn't have anything in the office to reflect his service. I asked if he had any photos to share, but I didn't receive a response. I thought that was a little odd, but I understood Vietnam was a difficult time for those war veterans.

Nevertheless, I didn't question his background at the time. Since there was nothing in the office to share his accomplishments, I asked a good friend from California, Matthew, to build a box from scratch. Matthew was very crafty when it came to woodwork. He and I met on the island and have kept in touch since.

I told Sam that a shadow box was being constructed for him. As the months went by, he began collecting his memorabilia. Some of the items he showed me didn't make sense. His ribbon rank consisted of enlisted army and air force basic training ribbons. I started to become suspicious of the legitimacy of his military career. He had every top medal an air force officer could have received—even a Purple Heart. I knew Purple Hearts were on record, but I found no Sam as a recipient of a Purple Heart. Despite these anomalies, I continued to build the box.

When it finally arrived, Matthew delivered it himself. It was good to meet his family and see a familiar face. People often ask me if I miss the military. My response is always no. I met some very good people while serving, but most of us still keep in touch to this day. I hold fast to those relationships and keep them close to my heart.

Now that the box had finally arrived, it was time to put it all together. That didn't take long. Unlike my shadow box, Sam's display was full. I mean, I thought my ribbon rack looked like a general, but his looked like five generals. There were red flags all over this thing. The dates alone triggered the first red flag. When I asked him if I could see his DD 214, he said he didn't have one. Anyone who retires from any branch of service will have a DD 214. This form identifies the type of service completed whether general, dishonorable, or honorable. When the box was finally completed, it was displayed in the office for all to see.

CHAPTER 6

# It Must Be Me

———

I joined the prayer team a few weeks after my arrival. The group was originally established a year before I arrived. While on the island, Sarah (not her actual name), the ministry lead, along with her husband, Sam (not his actual name), extended the invitation to participate with the prayer group, but my schedule didn't allow the time. Sarah, at times, mailed me packages consisting of the group's progress. Now that I was there, we dialed in with a provided conference call number every Wednesday evening. It consisted of people from all over the United States.

During the prayer meetings, I noticed Sam hardly prayed. I only remember one time when he did pray; it was a simple prayer like that of a child. Some of the prayers said were unusual to me. Sometimes, deep inside, it wouldn't settle my spirit. This was my first time being involved in a prayer line. It was nothing like I imagined it would be. Sarah led the prayers with the direction of Sam. I noticed prayers of destruction were often said; it would go from the evil, wicked spirit of the person prayed for, and then it would turn to attack the said person directly. This was another red flag. Our prayers shouldn't attack people. Our prayers should not bring harm to anyone. It was very dangerous if you ask me, and I was new to God's service. The Lord was teaching me. It wasn't right in my eyes. Destruction for people is not God's intention. God is love.

Recently, while reviewing my notes from that time, I found a statement I had recorded. This statement indicated that Chuck Norris accepted Christ through Sam. Chuck Norris recommended Sam for his deliverance. Those remarks didn't settle in my spirit. Even though I was receiving these checks in my spirit, I didn't have a concrete reason to distrust Sarah and Sam. I questioned the validity of my hesitation, particularly in light of my young walk with the Lord. What did I know? I saw Sam and Sarah as my spiritual father and mother, whom I love dearly. The Lord opened the door for me to come to this ministry through them. For this, I was most grateful. I honored them at all times through my words and deeds. I ignored the quiet voice within, which was telling me that things were not right.

The skills I learned while training in the military transferred well when I moved on to the ministry, especially when it came to character and behavior. I knew the Lord had put a new heart in me while I was in Afghanistan. Everything I had learned while serving in the Air Force, I was able to apply to ministry. Often, it was more spiritual than physical. I began learning about the Lord's army and quickly realized how similar it is to military life.

The biggest difference is the eternal perspective. Having an eternal mindset in the Lord's army is key to giving up one's life for another. I understood my sins were forgiven. I understood what the Lord did for me on the cross. I understood I am no longer a slave to sin but a co-laborer with Him to do those things that He desires of my life. I understood to obey the orders appointed over me. I understood He was first in my life, and I wanted more of Him. Everything I did now would be viewed by His nature, not my past nature. My sins are forgiven and washed by the blood of Jesus. Every thought, word, and deed became a reflection of the One who gave His life for me. He had my heart and my best interest in His hands.

Even though I started receiving multiple checks in my spirit, I was eager to learn through this prayer team. Some of the individuals who prayed were amazing, prayers of salvation and grace, and I loved to hear what they had to say. Even though I had not met them yet, my heart was already going out to them.

I recorded everything. I took as many notes as I could with an attentive heart. Sarah and Sam knew I took notes. The day after the prayer meetings, Sarah would have me type them up and ship them to each prayer member as a reminder of what had occurred during the meetings. It was here I began seeing how God's Word was used for destruction. Often, the contrast became apparent between what was said in these prayers and His written Word. I noticed what was manifesting from Sarah's heart just by what was said. God did not come to steal, kill, and destroy. He came that we might have life more abundantly:

> The thief cometh not, but for to steal, and to kill, and to destroy: I am come that they might have life, and that they might have it more abundantly. (John 10:10)

Everyone on the team trusted Sam and Sarah. We trusted their leadership and sound guidance when it came to the group. We had no reason to suspect any error from them; we loved them dearly. Our hearts were right toward them. My heart is still right toward them, but I knew deep down inside that something wasn't right. Unfortunately, being ignorant of the Word of God led me to follow suit.

One night, during a prayer session, it was briefed that Sam was to conduct President Trump's deliverance on *Air Force One*; he was going to lead him to the Lord. Leading anyone to the Lord is a burning desire in my heart. To me, it's like all of heaven rejoices in that one moment, the most important moment of their lives.

On an early morning in October, Sam was prepared for this trip to Washington DC. We met at the office, and someone called his cell phone to inform him the aircraft was ready for departure. I cannot tell you who that person was on the other line. All I can say is that before this, he said President Trump personally contacted him for deliverance. I did not witness the phone call or see an email or invitation from the president's staff. There is protocol when it comes to the matters of the president or any delegate in a position of authority, so I found it odd that there were no witnesses and no proof of this rare, esteemed invitation. That said, whatever Sam had on his calendar was not shared, and Sarah and I were never invited.

Sam was ready for departure. He had a small bag and was dressed up for the occasion. He drove himself to the local airport, and a private fighter jet, his mode of transportation, had been prepared for him. He said he was going to fly it himself.

I always enjoyed the sound of jet engines, especially on deployments. To me, it always signified America's freedom, power, and might. The roaring sound signifies a readiness for battle stance. Deep within me, I wanted to be there for takeoff. That morning, I wanted to hear them again. I was determined to hear them again.

Since he was departing on a fighter jet from the airport, which was a short distance away, I knew I would hear the jet engines once again. I waited and waited to hear from the ministry, even stepping outside to catch a glance. Nothing! I heard nothing. Nothing but the birds in the area.

I told myself it was no big deal. *I have heard many jets take off before.* I was just excited President Trump was about to receive Jesus. Many times, while Sam was away, Sarah and I enjoyed each other's company. She had lots of cats to tend to. When Sarah was with her cats, she was like a child. They were her pride and joy; they were her children. She loved them dearly. Together, we enjoyed what she loved: her cats.

Sam left that morning and returned in the evening. According to him, the president had indeed received Jesus into his heart. The meeting had been a success, but something wasn't sitting right with me. Why wasn't I as excited as they were? *My heart must not be right with the Lord*, I thought. *Something must be really wrong with me if I can't fully rejoice with Sarah and Sam on this victory.* I celebrated with them of course, but I wanted to put the pieces together that weren't adding up.

October was an eventful month for Sam. He had received a word from the Lord in the early morning hours entitled "The Trump Card." Everyone was excited to hear this prophecy from the Lord, given to Sam. It was anointed. It was the highlight of the prayer meetings. Everyone praised Sam for his amazing accomplishment.

Even though this did not settle in my mind as fact, I was convinced I needed deliverance. I directed my efforts to this over the upcoming holidays. I didn't think much of the deception that was manifesting at this ministry because they had been in ministry for years. *They must be right.* I reasoned that the Lord was working on me, revealing to me the shortcomings in my heart. I continued to have concerns about what was being said, all the while condemning the impurities that must exist in my heart for these doubts to persist.

I continued to serve the ministry faithfully. One of Sarah's books helped in my walk with the Lord. I respected her deeply. I was thankful to both of them for the opportunity to serve the Lord in their ministry for His service. I was genuinely convinced it was *me* who needed help and repentance.

The days grew colder and colder as we drew near the winter months. The home renovations were finally complete, and I felt settled in at last.

On a cold morning, after cleaning the kitty litter boxes, Sarah approached me with the most interesting topic: my husband. She said she had been praying for a husband for me. She asked me if it would be okay if she could continue to pray for my husband, injecting that he and I would inherit some things that the Lord has created in this ministry. She wasn't specific as to what we would inherit. There was no one to turn the ministry over to in order to continue God's work. If I didn't agree, she said, she would stop praying for him.

I did not give her an immediate response. I just listened to what she had to say. I am not quick to respond unless it's a life-threatening situation. I prefer involving the Lord in all my life's choices.

That evening, I took it the Lord. I asked Him if this was His will for me, then let be as she said. He knew my heart when it came to my future husband. With everything He had done for me, sending His only Son for me, my only desire was His presence. I wanted my husband, if I ever married, to be *from* Him. I cried out to the Lord for such a man, a man who feared the Lord, declaring we would forever praise His holy name all the days of our lives.

The Lord knows I have a burning desire to lead thousands and thousands of souls into the kingdom of God. That was my delight. These children of His will experience His love, His everlasting love, abiding in Him alone, delighting in Him alone, seeking His face until the ends of their earthly lives, for eternity. From there, I left it all in His hands. We never spoke of my husband again.

CHAPTER 7

# A New Year

———

Ever since I was born-again, I love to bring in the New Year with Jesus. My New Year's party usually consists of fasting and prayer. This particular New Year's, I had a sudden yearning to repent. I wanted things to be right between Him and me. Doing this always brought me joy. I get so much joy just spending time in His presence. This year, I cried out my prayer:

Lord Jesus,

I recognize that because of my covenant relationship with You, I have entered into combat with the kingdom of Satan. My first step is to declare absolute faithfulness to You. Father, my Lord, and Savior, my

King, I commit myself to You and Your leadership unconditionally, and I place my life fully in Your hands as Your Word affirms. I equip myself now with the full armor of God so I may stand victorious in this battle. I also pull down, in the name of Jesus, any strongholds or strong man in my life that deter me. Lord, help me in this battle, so I can follow You without hindrance.

Father, I remove any high place in my life that may obstruct me to old habits, to an old pattern, or religious practices of the churches I previously attended that may have been offensive to You. I repent! I lay it down now, Lord, and I place it at Your feet. I will join with my fellow believers in coming together into that secret place that God, the Father, has allowed for worship in the mighty and powerful name of Jesus.

Now, Lord, all that I am, and all that I have, I commit fully to You. I offer myself as one who will engage in spiritual warfare for the sake of Your kingdom, one who will pull down, destroy, and root out in Your name, not only individual strongholds, but also national ones. I will be one who removes the high places in my life and in the church's realm. Please use me for the sake of Your kingdom and Your eternal purpose. In Jesus's mighty name! Amen!

I was much better after this. I pressed forward each day with a diligence to serve God honorably and faithfully. I rested on all He had said to me in the past. These were the things I held dear to my heart. At times, they were all I had.

While serving at this ministry, daily I would claim:

> For the joy of the Lord is your strength. (Nehemiah
> 8:10)

I met Hanna at the ministry. Hanna use to be the local hairdresser. The ministry was located in a very small town away from everything. Hanna knew everyone. She and I bonded quickly. She was sweet, gentle, and very helpful when it came to the ministry. She and Sarah were very good friends. Before I came along, Hanna assisted Sarah with all the matters of the ministry. I was thankful the Lord sent me to help as well. Sarah needed a great deal of help. Sam rarely helped with anything unless it directly benefitted him. I noticed this at the turn into the New Year.

When Hanna came to the ministry, I was filled with joy. I spent my days alone at the office. I was the only employee at the ministry. I never understood that until Sarah told me about the many times they had been hurt by those who worked for them. They either stole money or were tempted to take over the ministry. Those thoughts never crossed my mind. I never wanted anything from anyone unless it came from Him directly. I knew all good things come from Him:

> Every good gift and every perfect gift is from above,
> and cometh down from the Father of lights, with
> whom is no variableness, neither shadow of turning.
> (James 1:7)

When anyone came to visit, I enjoyed good conversations. Hanna made the best hamburgers in the world. What I would do to have one of those burgers now! There were times Hanna would ask me if I believed everything Sam told me. I told her no. Some of the things he said were just over the top and impossible for any person's lifetime. He was the best golfer ever, he was an air force pilot who had been shot down in Vietnam, he was the rightful heir to England, he was in the police force *and* the Secret Service, and he dated Sally Field. I could go on and on.

Every now and then, Hanna would say, "You don't actually believe that, do you?"

I would give her a quiet look. I chose to focus on the good:

> Finally, brethren, whatsoever things are true, whatsoever things are honest, whatsoever things are just, whatsoever things are pure, whatsoever things are lovely, whatsoever things are of good report; if there be any virtue, and if there be any praise, think of these things. (Philippians 4:8)

Despite all the amazing experiences I'd had in the military, my main focus at that point in life was Jesus. He rightfully consumed my thought life.

One afternoon, while I was sitting in the office, I had a peculiar and very specific thought. I never spoke it or wrote it down. Quite simply, I wanted to see a deer up close. It wasn't until that evening while I was outside with my dog that a deer came from out of the woods not too far from me. It was here I that I understood: He knows my every thought before I even speak it.

> Thou knowest my downsitting and mine uprising, thou undestandest my thought afar off. (Psalm 139:2)

> For there is not a word in my tongue, but, lo, O Lord, thou knowest it altogether. (Psalm 139:4)

CHAPTER 8

# Flame of Fire

———

Two months into the year, I had a dream. While I was sleeping, I saw a bright light. It looked like a fire or a flame with all its colors. It remained lit for a few seconds, and then it moved like a bolt of lightning to my left hand. My left hand heated up, and I could feel the fire. The heat became unbearable, and I woke up from my sleep. It was so extreme. Even my dog, who slept right next to me, woke up, jumped off the bed, and puked. The moment I woke up, it was gone. Concerned that I was under a demonic attack, I cried out to the Lord and asked what that was:

> Heavenly Father,
> In Jesus's name, if this is from You, then let it be as
> You reveal it to be. If this is not from You, I rebuke

the enemy for what he has done. In Jesus's mighty name! Amen!

After my New Year's prayer, I realized where I worked and understood completely how the enemy might want to distort my thoughts. I asked the Holy Spirit to continue to guide me, lead me, and teach me through the Word of the Lord.

After the flame of fire, I felt a strange itch in the middle of the palm. On certain occasions, it felt like there was oil in it. It felt like a smoothness. I know an itch is not good just from what I have read in the Old Testament. In order to confirm what the oil actually felt like, I poured oil in the palm of my hand and moved it all around to determine its smooth texture. However, I continued to rebuke it, commanding whatever it was to go in Jesus's name.

Being around Sam and Sarah for almost seven months, they taught me that it was common to be attacked by the enemy. They shared that it was normal to have destruction around you. I never understood this. I knew my knowledge of the Word was elementary, but even *I* knew the Lord was love and not destruction. I knew we had authority over the enemy:

> Behold, I give unto you power to tread on serpents and scorpions, and over all the power of the enemy: and nothing shall by any means hurt you. (Luke 10:19)

Sam and Sarah claimed they were constantly attacked by the enemy. *Everything* that happened in their lives was regarded as an attack from the enemy. I rarely heard a praise report. This was very discouraging for me. I love to hear people's testimonies of how the Lord healed or delivered them from oppression. I loved to hear about miracles, signs, and wonders. It made my faith increase to hear of His glory.

In my quiet time, I continued to intercede for Sam and Sarah, but there never seemed to be a breakthrough. Nevertheless, I had that horrible itch in my left hand, and I needed to pursue the Lord to gain clarity and direction.

# Immediate Surgery

———

The next month, I lost my appendix. It began in the very early morning, just after one o'clock.

The first symptoms were extreme pains in my stomach area. I had never experienced that type of pain before. I broke into a fever, and my body was hit with waves of cold and hot flashes. I knew my body was breaking down; sweat combined with the chills was not a good sign. I alternated between cold and hot showers, and the fever finally subsided at about six in the morning. The pain was still intense, and I needed to get to the emergency room quickly.

Bent forward, barely able to stand, I wasn't able to drive myself to the ER. I started considering who I could call for help. I couldn't call the ministry; Sarah made it very clear to me not to call before eleven because Sam normally slept until then. I respected that. Most of the time, Sam worked until the early morning hours. An early-morning call would disturb his sleep.

I reached out to Hanna, but my call went straight to voice mail. With no one else to call, I stayed home and endured the pain until nine, which was when Hanna finally returned my call. She quickly picked me up, and that evening, I was rushed to the veterans hospital for immediate surgery. What a relief that was! Thank God for doctors. He has created doctors for a reason. Had it taken any longer, my appendix would have ruptured. Praise God!

Sam followed me to the hospital. It was very kind of him to be there during my surgery, and I was thankful for his presence.

For my recovery, Sarah and Sam allowed me to take as long as I needed. I took three days, and then I told them I could work, but I could not lift anything heavy. It was a quick recovery, but I still obeyed the doctor's orders. I had no interest in going through that type of pain again.

In 2004, I had cracked my tailbone while snowboarding in South Korea. That was bad, but this pain eclipsed that experience. After the surgery, I continued to work hard. I enjoyed everything I did for the ministry. Things just took me a little bit longer to complete.

CHAPTER 9

# Peace, Where
# Are You?

―

With all the attacks the ministry had been experiencing, I decided to study the conditions of peace for His righteous children. I knew that peace was the fruit of the Holy Spirit. The peace that had been planted within me grew into a redwood tree almost overnight when I was filled with the Holy Spirit while deployed in Afghanistan.

During our prayer meetings, I often wondered why there was never any peace at the White House. I directed most of my prayers that way. I wanted to know the conditions for peace. As I dove into the Word of the Lord, I discovered that one cannot have peace apart from righteousness. The conditions of peace can be found in Romans 14:17:

For the kingdom of God is not eating and drinking,
but righteousness, peace, and joy in the Holy Spirit.
(Romans 14:17)

To have peace, one must meet the conditions of righteousness. We
have all heard of Matthew 6:33:

But seek first the kingdom of God and his
righteousness, and all these things shall be added
unto you. (Matthew 6:33)

Peace is birthed in righteousness:

And the fruit of righteousness *is sown* in peace of
them that make peace. (James 3:18)

If we pursue righteousness, peace will grow from that righteous seed.
On the contrary, it is said in Isaiah 48:22:

There is no peace, says the Lord, for the wicked.
(Isaiah 48:22)

The Lord quickly revealed to me that apart from Jesus, there is no
peace. He is everlasting peace and everlasting joy, and those attributes
are found through righteousness. How exactly do we get this peace
in righteousness?

O that thou hadst hearkened to my commandants!
Then had thy peace been as a river, and thy
righteousness as the waves of the sea. (Isaiah 48:18)

The answer is simple and can be describe in one word: *obedience*. We must hearken to His commandments in obedience. God is desiring obedience. By obeying His commands, His ordinances, and His statutes, we can see the fruit of righteousness manifesting in our own lives, thus producing peace to make peace. Are we not told to pursue righteousness? Righteousness simply means in right standing with God. Nobody is perfect. There is nothing one can do that will make God love them less. There is nothing one can do that will make God love them more. He loves you unconditionally. Now we put on the mind of Christ pursuing love in everything. We must delight in it:

> But thou, O man of God, flee these things; and follow after righteousness, godliness, faith, love, patience, meekness. (1 Timothy 6:11)

I meditated on this for more than a month until His Word was in my spirit, identifying the conditions of peace and who they are reserved for. Peace is reserved for the righteous, those who manifest their love toward the Lord Almighty through their obedience. Now that I was able to understand the terms of peace for His children, I could discern how the enemy would make peace look possible, even preferable, aside from Jesus:

> There is a way which seemeth right unto a man, but the end thereof are the ways of death. (Proverbs 14:12)

Without Jesus and His righteousness, there will be a false peace, and many will be deceived. My faith in Jesus increased. He desires obedience. I wanted this peace to fall deeply upon our ministry. I hated for anyone to suffer within the ministry. I wanted to see Sarah healed and happy. I hated that this ministry was constantly being attacked.

## CHAPTER 10

# The Cry Out

———

M ay was going to be an exciting month for the prayer team. Before the end of the previous year, it was settled by all the members that we would meet in Jamestown, Virginia. We were going to walk and pray that land back to the Lord. Pastor Robert Hunt first dedicated Virginia to God in 1607. Our mission was to rededicate America and the church back to God. What better place to do that than in the same place where it all began? Everyone was ready to do some spiritual warfare. We had walked and prayed over the entire premises.

It was finally nice to see all the faces attached to the voices I'd heard during the prayer meetings. I got along with all of them. I could see their genuine love for the Lord and their desire to seek His face in diligence. There were people from all walks of life, and they all loved the Lord wholeheartedly.

It had been previously stated by Sam during a prayer meeting that we all would have an upper room experience at our Jamestown visit. Had His glory came, maybe some of us would have not made it through. Just like Ananias and Sapphira. The glory of the Lord filled the atmosphere that when Ananias stepped in it killed him, then his wife shortly thereafter. It isn't God's intention to kill anyone. He sent His Son so that the world might be saved through Him, giving life more abundantly. Nothing extravagant happened, and no miracles, signs, or wonders occurred, but what was about to happen changed my prayer life.

On the day we were all departing, while waiting in the front lobby for Sam and Sarah, one of the prayer team members turned and said, "Your appendix was demonic; seek God for discernment."

I was shocked. I looked her square in the eyes and replied, "I will."

Her remarks pressed on my heart, and I wanted the truth. Of all the things we had just accomplished, that one moment was the turning point in the ministry. Settling for constant demonic attacks is not from the Lord. He has given us His power, His might, His Word, His love, His nature, and His Son to defeat the enemy, and I needed to dive deep into the Word to find the truth. We are the victors through Christ Jesus!

Later that month, I cried out to God for discernment just like the woman had insisted I should at Jamestown. I asked the Lord for wisdom, understanding, and discernment years back, but that was nothing like this night.

I proclaimed:

Eternal Father,

This is my prayer to You genuinely. Lord Jesus, there are seven things You hate. Quicken my spirit, Lord, when these seven things are being practiced amongst

Your saints. Grant me discernment, wisdom, and understanding from above that I may know, Lord.

Your Word says, in Proverbs 8:13, that the fear of the Lord is to hate evil, pride, and arrogance. If it pleases the King, if I have found favor in Your sight, and these things seems right to You and I am pleasing in Your eyes, let it be so for me. Lord, You know I will obey You; lead me, Father. In Jesus's mighty name! Amen!

These six things doth the Lord hate: yea, seven are an abomination unto him: proud look, a lying tongue, and hands that shed innocent blood, a heart that deviseth wicked imaginations, feet that be swift in running to mischief, a false witness that speaketh lies, and he that soweth discord among brethren. (Proverbs 6:16–19)

The fear of the Lord is to hate evil: pride, and *arrogancy*, and the evil way, and the forward mouth, do I hate. (Proverbs 8:13)

Shortly thereafter this prayer, everything within the ministry began to heighten my attention. I fully understood the fruits of the Holy Spirit at the level I was spiritually, and Sam's characteristic traits and behaviors were not bearing the fruits of the Spirit. His behaviors were completely rotten, down to the roots. The entire tree would have to be torn down.

Displaying His nature in both character and behavior are the most important attributes in any Christian's walk. The Lord is more concerned about our character and behavior than He is about the gifts. It is here Christians will know them by their fruits, not by the gifts. The gifts of the Holy Spirit are just that: a gift from the Lord. People can operate in the gifts of the Holy Spirit but produce no fruit:

> For the gifts and the calling of God are irrevocable.
> (Romans 11:29)

God will not take back what He has freely given. One can operate fully in the gifts but hold a dark heart that is full of pride and selfishness. Jesus always looks to the heart. On the other hand, the fruits of the Spirit are what bring us to His likeness. What we do in our secret place will manifest through our actions. These good seeds of the Holy Spirit are planted and must be watered with the Living Word of the Lord for spiritual growth.

They way Sam treated his wife was the most obvious indicator to me that his relationship with the Lord was hindered in some way. It was not the behavior of a godly man. If fact, it displayed how much he lacked love and true reverence for the Lord. It completely broke my heart.

> Husbands, love your wives, even as Christ loved the
> church and gave himself for her. (Ephesians 5:25)

I'm no expert in marriage, but even *I* understood this passage. The husband's love for his wife should mirror that of Jesus's love for us: His church. He should serve and lead, laying down his life for her if needed. It's not a selfish love; it's pure, selfless service.

> Likewise, ye husbands, swell with them according to
> knowledge, giving honour until the wife, as unto the
> weaker vessel, and as being heirs together of the grace
> of life; that your prayers be not hindered. (1 Peter 3:7)

There was often mental abuse, and they had become isolated because of his actions. It was as if everyone was out to get them. They lived as if their lives were endangered. Reflecting back, this isolation was the first red flag. Christians should take caution when we separate ourselves from the body of Christ. We are bound to follow familiar spirits in isolation. There was no fellowship and no communion with like-minded folks.

The red flags were in every corner of the ministry. Everything Sam said left a question in my spirit. Nothing was settling. As I pressed deeper with the Lord, He began to teach me through the errors of the ministry. I had a desire to see through the bad and reflect on the good. I sought Him day and night for the things He was bringing forth to my attention, inquiring of my responsibility toward this knowledge.

CHAPTER 11

# The Bold Move

———

One day at the office, Sam and Sarah were in the best mood. It was refreshing to see them like that. Sam had just received another word from the Lord and asked if I could publish it on their website. I was delighted to do so.

Before publication, I took a quick glance at the text to catch any small grammatical errors. While I was reading, certain words lifted off the pages, just as they did when I was in Afghanistan. My spirit told me something was wrong. Soon, it became clear what the issue was: I sensed that the article was *not* written by Sam. Suddenly, I was nauseous. I began questioning what I saw and read.

That evening, I researched the article. Despite my suspicions, I was shocked when I found it online. It had been written by another author. I sat on my chair that evening and stared at the computer screen, trying not to believe what I'd just read. Then memories of all the other articles Sam had published began flowing through my mind. Since Sarah mailed all the articles ever published by him to the prayer team, I decided to check a few more—just to confirm the extent of his plagiarism.

I found a majority the articles he'd shared on the internet, yet again, written by someone else. I battled with this knowledge day and night until I'd finally had enough of the torment. It had begun building up inside of me. Being in the military, I know not to disrespect leadership. We are taught to obey those appointed over us during basic training. And this, my friends, *was* basic training. Even in the Lord's ministry, there is basic training. One should not react to a situation like this with emotions. I knew I had to turn this over to the Lord and ask for His discernment in the next steps.

> Humble yourselves therefore under the mighty hand
> of God, that he may exalt you in due time: Casting all
> your care upon him; for he careth for you. (1 Peter 5:7)

By the end of June, I'd finally had enough. I'd gathered more than enough evidence to know that Sam was not being truthful. I fell to my face and cried out to the Lord:

> Eternal Father,
>
> I come boldly to Your throne, presenting this case of
> deception. Lord, You have been faithful in quickening
> me when things aren't of You, and I thank You and
> You alone, Father.
>
> You have brought to my attention a few articles by
> Sam that aren't from him. I noticed the gray spaces on

the document that instantly led me to believe it was copied. Lord, I know what Your Word says about lies; You hate them, and they are not from You (Proverbs 6; John 8:44). Tell me, Lord Jesus, what am I to do? Guide me, I will obey Father.

Lord, I ask that You protect me with Your angels as I do this; a special hedge of protection, Father. Lord, please help me with this. You brought Leviticus 19:19 to my attention this week. I believe You are preparing me, Father. I am listening! In Jesus's name, amen!

Lord, I return with Your Word, which never returns void. Father, you know the things I need before I ask You. Your will come, Your kingdom come. Let the truth be revealed; darkness must come to the light, Your light, Lord Jesus. Open the eyes of all those who view these evil things (directed to the prayer team members). Pour Your Spirit out, Lord, that they may see and have ears to hear. I put on Your full armor of God permanently this day forward. Encamp me with Your angels. You have said to me when I arrived here that no harm shall come to me. I rest on Your Word spoken to me. I rebuke the Spirit of fear, intimidation, murder, lust, anger, lying, all in Jesus's name. Lord, shut them up now; shut their mouths as You deal with Your saints to defeat the enemy. You say in Your Word in Proverbs 6:19 that You hate a false witness who speaks lies and feet that are swift in running to evil. I cried out to you for discernment, wisdom, and understanding. You have answered my prayer. Show me what I am to do now. Guide me, Father.

Eternal Father, I need Your help. I need You and You alone more than ever now. I submit myself to you fully at this hour and all my days. The joy of the Lord is my strength. Embrace me with Your everlasting arms, secured in Your bosom, Lord. Quicken me before an enemy attack that I may respond swiftly and in Your power, Your Son's power. I ask all this in Jesus's name. Amen! Lord, I know that You are the only One who can judge a man's heart. "Therefore, judge nothing before the time, until the Lord comes, who will both bring to light the hidden things of darkness and reveal the counsels of the hearts" (1 Corinthians 4:5) I cast this case before You, Lord. I do not want to dishonor anyone, Lord. In Jesus's name! Amen.

> Ye shall know them by their fruits. Do men gather grapes of thorns, or figs of thistles? (Matthew 7:16)

> Therefore, judge nothing before the time, until the Lord come, who both will bring to light the hidden things of darkness and will make manifest the counsels of the hearts: and then shall every man have praise of God. (1 Corinthians 4:5)

> Blessed are ye, when men shall revile you, and persecute you, and shall say *all manner of* evil against you falsely, for my sake. Rejoice and be exceeding glad: for great is your reward in

heaven: for so persecuted they the prophets *which* were before you. (Matthew 5:11–12)

Ye are of your father the devil, and the lusts of your father ye will do. He was a murderer from the beginning, and abode not in the truth, because there is no truth in him. When he *speaketh* a lie, he *speaketh* of his own: for he is a liar, and the *father of it*. (John 8:44)

Ye shall keep my statutes. Thou shalt not let thy cattle gender with a diverse kind: thou shalt not sow thy field with mingled seed: neither shall a garment mingled of linen and woolen come upon thee. (Leviticus 19:19)

More than ever before, I pressed in to seek His face diligently as to what He wanted me to do. I waited patiently for His direction in faith so that He would lead me to the right path. I know the Lord is faithful and has my best interests at heart.

In early summer, one crisp early morning at about two o'clock, I received an open vision. I was wide-awake, unable to sleep, and I was accelerating very quickly. As I was pushing through with great speed, I heard jet engines, but there were no jets. I could see trees surrounding me with the most vibrant reds and oranges. I couldn't tell if the gray road was paved or covered in stone. When I stopped at the end of the road, I saw the most beautiful redwood trees I had ever seen. Before this vision came to me, I sensed the Holy Spirit in my bedroom. His presence filled the atmosphere with such peace and joy.

At four o'clock that afternoon, the interpretation came forth. With a humbled heart, I realized the Lord's message:

I will exalt you above others very soon, hence the
speed. You have taken the narrow road, not many
have or are on this path. You are not alone at the
end of this journey; I will be with you till the end of
this age.

That encounter was all I needed to hear to press forward and bring
forth the deception to Sam and Sarah. It encouraged me to move
boldly. I waited patiently and humbled myself unto the Lord, and He
spoke clearly on that day.

Humble yourselves therefore under the mighty hand
of God, that he may exalt you in due time: Casting all
your cares upon him; for he careth for you. (1 Peter
5:6–7)

Because strait is the gate, and narrow is the way,
which leadeth unto life, and few there be that find it.
(Matthew 7:14)

Whom shall I send, and who will go for us? Then said
I, Here am I; send me. (Isaiah 6:8)

Teaching them to observe all things that I have
commanded you; and lo, I am with you always, even
to the end of the age. (Matthew 28:20)

My sheep hear my voice, and I know them, and they
follow me: And I give unto them eternal life; and they
shall never perish, neither shall any man pluck them
out of my hand. (John 10:27–28)

The very next day, without hesitation, I addressed all of the deceptions to Sarah. I explained and showed the evidence that the Lord had revealed to me. We talked about the issue for about an hour.

After our discussion, she didn't stay long at the office. She was very frail and weak as well. A major accident before I arrived at the ministry had completely shattered her clavicle. There were many days she didn't report for work because of that. I strongly wanted to take care of her at her home, but I only entered when I was invited to do so. The Lord had shown me the reason her bones would not heal, and that broke my heart as well. It was because of a broken spirit:

> A merry heart doeth good like a medicine: but a broken spirit drieth the bones. (Proverbs 17:22)

Her bones were practically hollowed and unable to heal. I believe the only love Sarah received at home was from her cats. My heart was breaking for her, and there was nothing I could do. I remained obedient in my service to them both.

On that day, everything changed at the ministry. Even with the vision and its clear message, I started to question whether I had done the right thing. That night, in my quiet time with my Father in heaven, the following just flowed out of me:

> Today, I spoke to Sarah about the things discovered on Friday. I provided all the evidence to her and explained how I recognized that the last piece posted on the website was not written by Sam. I thought a retaliation or heavy argument was about to occur, but oddly, it did not. Sarah was very calm. That was one of the hardest things I've ever had to do. I can't

tell you how difficult this was for me because I loved them both so dearly. We talked on the topic for about an hour. She mentioned how for all who worked for them, Sam had created a stumbling block in their faith with Christ. God pronounces a woe on those who cause one of His little ones to stumble.

Woe whoso shall offend one of these little ones which believe in me, it were better for him that a millstone were hanged about his neck, and that he were drowned in the depth of the sea. (Matthew 18:6)

Fervently, I prayed for Sarah:

Eternal Father, You are a good God. Our strength, peace, and joy come from You and You alone. Lord, grant Sarah wisdom, understanding, and knowledge from You. You are our Provider. Give her strength like David when he defeated Goliath. Guide her through all this so that she may rise *up* to defeat this giant she has been battling since she married. Encamp her, Lord, with Your angels of fire, that no harm shall come to her physically, mentally, or spiritually. Extend Your everlasting arm to her now, for she is the victor in Christ Jesus. Lord, grant Sam Your grace so that he may see his errors and repent of them. Touch his heart, Lord, as You have never done before in anyone. For I know You will restore all that the enemy has stolen in this union if he repents. May Your everlasting peace and joy be with Sarah as she goes through this difficult time. Let the words of the enemy bounce off her, for she has Your armor on, Lord. Let those fiery arrows miss her. Lord, let peace reign again in the heart of Sam. Let love be the centerfold of his works. Let Your love reach even unto the darkest places of Sam's heart, for Your love is everlasting and able to penetrate through the darkness. Lord, I ask all this in Your Son's mighty powerful name: Jesus Christ! Amen! Cover Sarah with *Your* blood! Your blood flows through her veins. Your Word has entered the depths of her heart. Heaven and earth shall pass away, but Your Word will remain forever. Amen!

That evening, before I shut my eyes for bed, thoughts about whether I had done the right thing began to enter my head.

Suddenly, a gentle voice said, "I see My Son in you."

I wept like a child and declared, "I commit myself this day to You, Lord, who judges righteously."

> Who, when he was reviled, reviled not again; when he suffered, he threatened not; but committed himself to him that judgeth righteously. (1 Peter 2:23)

I claimed Psalm 91 over my bones and my life, and I prayed. "I welcome Your Holy Spirit this day. I submit myself afresh in unreserved obedience to You. Your will come, Your kingdom come. Today, I fast, Lord, for Sarah, for Devine intervention."

> For our light affliction, which is for a moment, *worketh* for us a far more *exceedingly* and eternal weight of glory. (2 Corinthians 4:17)

"Father, please send Your angels quickly to protect her. That the mouth of all those mixed spirits in Sam will be silent in Jesus's name. Stand firm, Sarah. In Jesus's name!"

The voice said, "Protect My sheep! Protect My sheep!"

I didn't think too much about what I was hearing at the time.

I continued to stay hidden in Christ. The next day, while driving into the ministry, I noticed many spiders in their webs along the road. I'm sure the webs had been there the whole time, but I was just able to see them then. Since it was a holiday, I didn't stay long at the ministry.

On my drive home, at 8:34 a.m., the voice of the Lord said, "Protect My Sheep! Protect My Sheep! The lies are being exposed into the light just like you saw all the spider webs exposed by the morning dew, reflecting the light. So, I am exposing the wicked ways of the enemy. You have asked this from me. He is full of pride, anger, and arrogance. My fear is not in him. If he does not repent, his place is Sheol."

I knew the Lord wanted to restore the ministry, but repentance must come first. When I heard, "My fear is not in him," it was over for me at the ministry. There was no way I could serve in that ministry any longer. What is one to do when they lack the Fear of the Lord? This is the beginning of it all. This is the foundation, along with His love, that must be taught when receiving the milk as a babe in Christ. It is a key element in anyone's walk with Jesus Christ. This was all I needed to hear.

> The fear of the Lord is the beginning of wisdom: and the knowledge of the holy is understanding. (Proverbs 9:10)

On that day, I cried out to the Lord for the protection of His sheep:

> You have said in Your Word to protect Your sheep, the flock. You have charged me, Lord, with Your precious

words written in 2 Timothy 4. I am listening, Father, to all You say, do, and show me. I am *Your* servant.

For our light affliction, which is but for a moment, worketh for us a far more exceeding and eternal weight of glory. (1 Corinthians 4:17)

I helped Sarah with the chickens that morning. I enjoyed feeding them daily. Sarah came to me and said, "Regarding the prophecy that states 'The Trump Card.' Sometimes Sam shares his writings with people. Since Sam has a photographic memory, I wonder if he might write things without even realizing he mentally photographed the message from someone else on a previous date."

My heart broke again for this woman. She wanted to believe her husband was not deceptive. Her mind was looking for ways to wash him of his guilt.

I stood in truth, but I delivered it gently. I replied, "Yes, ma'am. Both could be true, but having a photographic memory, you can also recall the source from which you memorized something. Sharing your writings is good, but another individual published the Trump prophecy in his own name. Wouldn't this make the original writer upset that his words were taken?"

She gave no response to that question. At that point, all I could hear were the bird chirps and the locusts; there was complete silence between the two of us. After a few moments, she walked away.

As the days passed, I continued putting on my full armor of God, asking for protection, and ministering the angels to surround me. I constantly rebuked all curses or any witchcraft that would try to influence me or hurt me in any way. I continually pleaded, "The joy of the Lord is my strength," claiming His Word that no harm would come to me.

The Lord had told me that no harm would come to me, and I claimed that earnestly. With my military background in combat training, I knew I was on dangerous grounds. I was no fool to warfare. Because of my background, I grasped onto spiritual warfare, remaining vigilant and alert. All that I had learned in the natural realm while serving, I was able to apply in the spiritual realm. I paid close attention to His Word when He spoke of war.

Weeks went by, and there were still no signs of a repentant heart within Sam. To be honest, I wasn't expecting any. None of it was about me. I had experienced brokenness in Afghanistan. There is a complete surrender when someone hits that point in their lives. It's like you're all in for Him unto death, and there is no turning back. Why would anyone want to turn away from the Lord after being in His presence?

Out of nowhere, Sam had a vision. In this vision, he planned to purchase Hanna's salon and create a teaching center. He wanted to conduct Bible studies, and he asked if I would conduct self-defense classes regarding spirituality.

Ideas flowed back and forth in my mind with endless possibilities. I told him I would have to take it to God before I agreed to anything. I was on a constant guard. They were not my enemy. No one is really your enemy when you are centered in Christ for His perfect will, perfect plan, and perfect purpose. The desire is repentance. You want to see them turn to Christ, not wanting anyone to perish, and everyone to come to repentance.

The longer I stayed, the closer I grew to the Lord. I would just be still and know that He is God, and He is in complete control of the situation.

> Be still, and know that I am God: I will be exalted
> among the heathen, I will be exalted in the earth.
> (Psalm 46:10)

While I was in my quiet time with the Lord, James 3:18 would come back to my thoughts:

> Now the fruit of righteousness *is sown* in peace by those who make peace. (James 3:18)

During this time, I recalled the note a friend had written for me at the beginning of the year: "The manifestation of the Lord is peace."

As the Lord had revealed His wisdom on the deception within the ministry, I had no peace in my heart depart yet. The Lord knew my heart. I was ready to leave, but I was not going to depart until He said it was time. I didn't want to leave the ministry that way, knowing very well the next time something like that happened, it would be easier to depart without closure. I needed the Lord to release me.

I knew I was called to that ministry for a purpose, and the Lord showed me that purpose: repentance. This was His heart for this ministry. I was full of love and compassion to rebuild and restore this ministry. He desired to restore that ministry to prepare it for the greatest miracle the world would ever see: the greatest revival where thousands upon thousands upon thousands enter into the kingdom of God. We weren't ready for that yet. The church must be ready for an influx of people entering into its doors.

I continued to serve the ministers faithfully and honorably in all things. As the days continued, the Lord's angels ministered to me on false prophets. Scriptures such as Joshua 13:22 and Acts 16 were pressed on my heart. Balaam desired gain and profit. Joshua 13:22 describes Balaam as a soothsayer. I've learned from the Lord that truth is not just a repetition of words but its transformation in our actions, a heart attitude as life happens. I asked the Lord to continue to teach me through His Word and give me courage and strength to stand against any giant, just like King David.

> Balaam also the son of Beor, the soothsayer, did the children of Israel slay with the sword among them that were slain by them. (Joshua 13:22)

Every night, I continued to thank Him for all He was doing with me. He was teaching me in His character and behavior, and I needed Him more than ever. I understood He was teaching and molding me in character and behavior in His love, mercy, and compassion.

It was His heart for all to turn to Him. Hell was not made for you; it was made for the devil and his cohorts. I was reminded of King David. He spent years being hunted by King Saul. I believe that during those tough times when David was in hiding, the Lord was building him up to become a great leader. David never hurt Saul. He never laid a hand on Him. He knew not to touch the Lord's anointed. You do not touch those the Lord has appointed.

I got down on my face and cried out:

> Heavenly Father, eternal God, Lover of my soul, I come before You naked, submitted unto Your righteous authority. Lord, I will wait upon You. I will be still in You on what I am to do regarding all that has been exposed. I need You, Lord. Hear my cry. Tell me what I am to do. I will obey. I will do as You command. My heart seeks You and You alone. You make my crooked paths straight. You make all things new (1 Samuel 3:1). I have repented of a few words that came to me, and I realized that I will not hurt Your anointed again (Psalm 105:15). Protect my

heart from the enemy. May he not penetrate my heart for it belongs to You. I claim Isaiah 54:17, which states that no weapon formed against me shall prosper, and every word that rises up against me I condemn it now, in Jesus's name. My righteousness is from You, O Lord of Host, this is my heritage. In Jesus's name. Amen!

CHAPTER 12

# Waiting upon the Lord

———

I enjoyed the times when the Lord sent His ministry angels to help me grow in His stature and nature. There were many times in the evenings, while at home, I would catch a glimpse of lights like silhouettes. There were many. I asked the Lord, "Are these angels waiting for a command?" I knew they were there with me.

> For he shall give his angels charge over thee, to keep
> thee in all thy ways. (Psalm 91:11)

I knew He went before me. When I stepped onto the ministry grounds, I sensed a great anger filling the atmosphere, even when I was near Sam. Things were a bit peculiar, but the Lord kept me in His everlasting arms. I had the peace that passes all understanding.

In July, I began reading 1 Samuel 3:1–18 at work:

> And the child Samuel ministered unto the Lord before Eli. And the word of the Lord was precious in those days. And it came to pass at that time, when Eli was laid down in his place, and his eyes began to wax dim, that he could not see; And ere the lamp of God went out in the temple of the Lord, where the ark of God was, and Samuel was laid down to sleep; That the Lord called Samuel: and he answered, Here am I. And he ran unto Eli, and said, Here am I; for thou calledst me. And he said, I called not; lie down again. And he went and lay down. And the Lord called yet again, Samuel. And Samuel arose and went to Eli, and said, Here am I; for thou didst call me. And he answered, I called not, my son; lie down again. Now Samuel did not yet know the Lord, neither was the word of the Lord yet revealed unto him. And the Lord called Samuel again the third time. And he arose and went to Eli, and said, Here am I; for thou didst call me. And Eli perceived that the Lord had called the child. Therefore, Eli said unto Samuel, Go, lie down: and it shall be, if he call thee, that thou shalt say, Speak, Lord; for thy servant heareth. So Samuel went and lay down in his place. And the Lord came, and stood, and called as at other times, Samuel, Samuel. Then Samuel answered, Speak; for thy servant heareth. And the Lord said to Samuel,

Behold, I will do a thing in Israel, at which both the ears of everyone that heareth it shall tingle. In that day I will perform against Eli all things which I have spoken concerning his house: when I begin, I will also make an end. For I have told him that I will judge his house for ever for the iniquity which he knoweth; because his sons made themselves vile, and he restrained them not. And therefore I have sworn unto the house of Eli, that the iniquity of Eli's house shall not be purged with sacrifice nor offering for ever. And Samuel lay until the morning, and opened the doors of the house of the Lord. And Samuel feared to shew Eli the vision. Then Eli called Samuel, and said, Samuel, my son. And he answered, Here am I. And he said, What is the thing that the Lord hath said unto thee? I pray thee hide it not from me: God do so to thee, and more also, if thou hide any thing from me of all the things that he said unto thee. And Samuel told him every whit, and hid nothing from him. (1 Samuel 3:1–18)

My thoughts pondered Samuel's character as a boy under the leadership of Eli, who had wicked sons. Instead of exposing their errors and sinful natures, Samuel ministered to the Lord before Eli. Samuel's encounter with the Lord allowed him to grow in obedience to wait upon the Lord's direction about when to release the word given to him. I now understood with more depth than ever how that was no easy task. We never want to hurt those we love, but God's love is greater. God sees the outcomes; God sees the end. His purpose is an eternal one. We are to seek His perfect righteousness.

I knew the Lord was teaching me to protect those around me. Not even my family knew what was going on with me at the ministry. I protected this situation from any other wicked schemes or attacks that would fall upon me. I wasn't going to cause anyone to feel distrust toward Sam or Sarah. I completely surrendered it all to the Lord. I rested on His Word and His spoken words to me. I didn't want to be like the others who had worked at the ministry. Looking back now, they probably had done exactly what I had just done. I let go and let God!

When Eli asked Samuel what the Lord had said to him, only then did he say the truth. It wasn't by correction. Most people would have either left the church or ran to expose the error before seeking God's guidance and direction.

As I meditated on these scriptures and the actions of Samuel, a gentle voice said, "I am quite capable of handling My own children."

Not quick to respond back, I pondered what had just been spoken. In a delayed response, I humbly replied, "Yes, Lord. You are very capable of handling Your own."

From this alone, I knew not to touch His anointed. I prayed blessings for Sarah and Sam.

> Saying, Touch not mine anointed, and do my prophets
> no harm. (Psalm 105:15)

Things weren't the same around the ministry. I rarely saw Sam. I continued to serve them as though I served unto the Lord, touching not His anointed ones. This was His ministry, and He desired to restore it.

While I was preparing welcome packages for three new prayer members, Sarah came in and said that the Lord had rebuked her for covering the titles on all the prophecies by Sam but written by another. Just the day before, she had told me to cover all the articles with a new label, removing Sam's name as the author. I didn't ask her what the Lord did or said to her about why we were to remove the labels she had asked me to create, "A Word from the Lord," but thoughts about the prayer team flooded my mind.

If the prophecies were mailed with the new label, a member of the team who was good friends with the new members might notice the anomaly and bring it up during the prayer meeting, which would unveil the truth.

The Lord knows all things. He continued to guard my heart, not allowing the enemy to penetrate my thoughts as well. He kept me in His everlasting arms, knowing He would be glorified in all this. One cannot trust a lie, hoping to get the truth from it. The Lord does not build on deception. If anyone thinks they are going to grow in Christ based on lies, then there was never any truth in them. That ministry was operating on deception. I strongly believe it wasn't like that in the beginning. I believe Sarah was on fire for the Lord. The hand of the Lord was upon that place. The enemy crept in and began to steal, kill, and destroy that which was once good.

As the days went by, conversation became scarce at the ministry. Often, I was the only one working in the office. I would just pray. I prayed over everything that came to mind. I prayed over the prayer basket that had rarely been prayed over since I had been at the ministry. I stood firm and remained hidden in Christ, yearning for repentance.

Toward the end of July, after being alone for many days, Sam came through the doors early one morning. I said hi to him, and that was about it. About ten minutes went by before he said anything. I knew he had something to say, and I waited patiently for a response.

He said, "If I made you mad, forgive me."

I looked him straight in the eye, but I wasn't quick to reply. So many thoughts flowed through my mind. The Lord says we are to forgive:

> Then came Peter to him, and said, Lord, how oft shall my brother sin against me, and I forgive him? Till seven times? Jesus saith unto him, I say not unto thee, Until seven times: but Until seventy times seven. (Matthew 18:21–22)

Because of what Jesus did for me on the cross, I knew in my heart that I had to forgive him:

> For if ye forgive men their trespasses, your heavenly Father will also forgive you: But if ye forgive not men their trespasses, neither will your Father forgive your trespasses. (Matthew 6:14–14)

After a long pause, I said, "We are good, Sam. Forgive me. I forgive you." In my heart, I knew his apology was not genuine. I wanted to cry. I wanted to leave right then and there. *I am not the one he needs to ask forgiveness of; it's the Lord*, I thought. As for me, I forgave him.

Because of everything that had unfolded, in my heart, I could no longer believe anything from Sam. Our conversation was short. It didn't take long for him to start back up again. He talked about an individual who had bought some land near the property where I was living. This person bought the land just up the mountain from where I stayed, which was by a major road. Sam said that the man wanted to build a road that would lead to the hill where his other renters lived. Sam continued to say how this man had made a few folks mad about the road that led to the property. Because of this, the man could not use the roadway by the local store that belonged to a well-known company. The bridge off the main road was the only road that he could use to get to his property on the mountain.

The motives of Sam's heart were deceitful, and I continued to seek the Lord for discernment and the wisdom to see beyond my human thinking and see through the lens of Jesus Christ.

> For my thoughts are not your thoughts, neither are your ways my ways, saith the Lord. (Isaiah 55:8)

> Casting down imaginations, and every high thing that exalteth itself against the knowledge of God, and bringing into captivity every thought to the obedience of Christ. (2 Corinthians 10:5)

This was a strange conversation, random for sure. I had met this man when I arrived at the ministry. We had talked for a bit, but he mostly wanted to know why I was working for the ministry.

His side of the story reflected the opposite of what I had just heard from Sam. The roles were reversed. Sam was the angry one. I heard both sides of the story; discerning it was Sam creating the division and making up lies to make himself look good.

After that day, I rarely saw Sam or Sarah. I love the Lord with all my heart, and I want to serve Him and know Him intimately. Even through all this, I wanted to see a breakthrough. But there was none; there was no change of heart.

CHAPTER 13

# The Smooth Stone

———

Pressing deeper into the Lord, I asked Him to help Sarah and me defeat these giants within the ministry—just like David did with Goliath.

In a conversation with my sister's mother-in-law, I heard myself saying, "I am the stone being thrown to defeat Goliath." There was a quench of the Holy Spirit at the ministry meaning He was nowhere to be found. Surely the beginning of this ministry had been better than its ending.

> Then he took his staff in his hand and he chose for himself five stones from the brook and put them in a shepherd's bag, in a pouch which he had, and his sling was in his hand. And he drew near to the philistine. (1 Samuel 17:40)

The end of a thing is better than its beginning.
(Ecclesiastes 7:8)

That's God's Word. When I first accepted Jesus as my Lord and Savior, I understood my ending will be greater than my beginning. When I was in the military, I always wanted to leave the work center I worked at better than how I found it. I wanted to leave better than when I arrived. I never wanted to remain the same. I always wanted to grow in leadership.

God is infinite. He is everlasting to everlasting. He is limitless. That is the God I serve, and I want all that He has planned for my life. We all have a calling on our lives, and in our intimate relationships with Him, He is willing to reveal it to us. He is looking for obedience.

I loved Sam and Sarah with all my heart. I still love them to this day. So, I continued to fight in the Spirit. I continued to intercede for them, rebuking the attacks of the enemy and the spirit of anger, jealousy, power, greed, coveting, pride, and dishonesty. I was becoming stronger in the Lord and resting on His promises as I continued to fight this fight. Every day, I was clothing myself with His zeal, vengeance, and humility, and then I put on the full armor of God. He promised no harm would come to me. His Word did not return void.

Time pressed forward, and during a prayer meeting, Sarah reminded everyone of a prophecy Sam had received not too long ago that talked about what God was going to do with the United States. She told us not to be dismayed. She stated that what was going on with the House of Representatives had just kicked off his prophecy. There was just one problem with that. The prophecies were not Sam's. Once again, Sam had copied them from another source on the internet, claiming them to be his own.

Therefore, behold, I am against the prophets, saith
the Lord, that steal my words everyone from his
neighbour. (Jeremiah 23:30)

Lord, have mercy on us all. When I heard this, I wanted to speak up
and reveal it all. It wasn't in my nature to do so. I'm not one to cause
division. Instead, I decided to leave the phone on mute and just walk
away to calm myself down. It was frustrating to hear the deception
spoken to all those tentative sheep, and they believed every word
that she said. They had no reason to doubt Sarah or Sam, but I knew
the truth. I wanted to do God's perfect will and fulfill what He has
called me to do there. I knew no change of heart would take place.
Sarah *enabled* her husband by agreeing to the deception and not
correcting it.

In the middle of August, for the first time since I had joined the
prayer team, I was disconnected from the call. As I looked at the
"call failed" message displayed on my cell phone, I felt peace flowing
from the top of my body to my feet. In that moment, I knew I had
just received confirmation from the Lord that I was set to depart the
ministry. Through everything that had recently occurred—all the
lies and deception—I could not stay and be a part of that ministry.

There were two ways I could have responded is. First, I could
have tried to see the good and focus on that, thereby accepting the
lies. The second option would be to focus on the error, but then I
would be rejecting the good. In either case, it would not accomplish
God's purpose. This would only lead to confusion and, ultimately,
division. My thinking would become thwarted in the Lord. I couldn't
reason myself into staying, which I did with Kevin. A lie will never
become truth. God does not build on deception. He is truth.

Your Word is truth. (John 17:17)

Truth will never come from lies. I didn't know what was ahead once I departed. All I knew for certain was that I would leave it all up to God. I am fully His for His service. When trials or tribulations happen in a person's life, how they respond determines the outcome. We have one meaningful choice at these forks in the road: *Do I give it to God or try to handle it myself?* The response begins with a thought, and then it will form words, which ultimately become our actions. The more challenges that arose, the deeper I dove into the Word of God.

With the peace to depart, I prepared for that day. I didn't let Sam or Sarah know of my plans just yet. I continued to serve them faithfully in all things they asked me to do. No complaining or murmuring ever escaped my lips. I knew better than to do those things.

CHAPTER 14

# The Departure Letter

---

Sarah must have briefed the prayer team that I was no longer a part of the meetings. I had asked to be removed. A few members of the prayer team had reached out to me to ask if I was okay.

Montana was dear to my heart, and she often called in the evenings to fellowship. Our conversations were pleasant, deep, and spiritual. She asked if was okay. I told her I was okay and that I could not share any information right then about why I had left the team. She respected that.

Before the summer ended, I wanted to let the ministry know I was departing. I wrote a letter to explain why I was leaving in the simplest way I could. Since no one showed up at the ministry that day, I placed it on top of the keyboard for both of them to see. I had to make sure they would see it.

Dear Sam and Sarah,

I want to take this time to let both of you know that I will depart the ministry most likely in the first week of October unless God deems sooner. I write these words in love, peace, and complete obedience to the Lord. Please allow me to explain.

Since early June, I have earnestly sought God on all things pertaining to what was revealed. In the beginning, it was difficult to determine what was true and what wasn't. I would often ask myself, Is this a half-truth or the whole truth? I could focus on the good, thereby accepting the error, or I could focus on the error, rejecting the truth. Either way, it would not accomplish God's purpose.

I had to rebuke this spirit of confusion. Soon after, I brought into captivity every thought to the obedience of Christ. Now more than ever, I have this deep desire within me to depart, which I know the Lord has placed there. I have laid all this at His feet, and He has heard my cries. The evening before I asked to be removed from the prayer team, while listening in, my connection failed immediately after I heard Sarah refer to an old prophecy.

For the first time since I joined the prayer team, I saw "call failed" displayed on my phone and could not dial back in. The Lord did not permit it. I know the Lord is working in me in the development of His fruits for spiritual maturity. That is my heart's desire: His fruits in character and behavior.

Not even seconds later, peace flowed through my entire body, and I immediately knew it was time for me to leave. It's time. In the matter that was presented back in June, the Lord took me to the Old Testament recordings in the life of Samuel. I love what is written in 1 Samuel 3:1: "Now the boy Samuel ministered to the Lord before Eli." This is exactly how I approached the everlasting God. This isn't an offense or an attack by Satan. I am not here to cause division. It deals with repentance. I can't compromise or be passive when it comes to the Word of God. God does not test us with evil; He tests us with obedience.

For the past several months, the Lord has led me through each day, revealing Himself more clearly through His Word. With the fear of the Lord and trembling at His Word, He has indicated to me that He is quite capable of handling His own. This left me speechless. My delayed response came minutes later as I sat and pondered on this. "Yes, Lord, You are very capable of handling Your own," I humbly declared.

I will continue to do the things you ask of me and serve you faithfully. If a new person is hired, I will be more than happy to train him or her. I do pray for your health, wealth, and continued success in the ministry. I depart in peace and with joy.

From my heart, thank you for everything.

After this was done, I cried out to the Lord, trembling at what had just happened:

Lord, You know what I have done today. This day was written in Your book before the foundations of the earth. You knew every detail, every moment of its dwelling, before it came to play. You knew Sam and Sarah would not be in the office today. You knew I would tell them I am leaving the ministry today. You knew I would end up leaving the letter I wrote in plain sight so they could find it and read it. Lord, it's done; it's finished. I have said what You wanted me to say, and I have done all that You have commanded me to do. In the beginning, You guided me through Your Word that I am to do all they say like Joseph did in Potiphar's house. I have done just that. I hope it pleased the King in my actions and deeds. Right now, Lord, I rest on Your Word yet again, the same Word You gave to me for the son of a prayer team member from 1 Peter 3:16 (suffering for righteousness): "Having a good conscience, that when they defile you as evil does those who revile your conduct in Christ may be ashamed."

"Blessed are you when they revile and persecute you, and say all kinds of evil against you falsely for My namesake. Rejoice and be exceedingly glad, for great is your reward in heaven, for so they persecuted the prophets who were before you" (Matthew 5:11–12). Lord, I also declare that greater is He who is in me than he who is in the world (1 John 4:4). Lastly, Titus 2:7–8, in all things showing yourself to be a pattern of good works in doctrine showing integrity, reverence, incorruptibility, sound speech, the one who is an opponent be ashamed, having nothing evil to say of you. Father, I praise Your Holy name, Jesus Christ, forever and ever. Flood the hearts within this

ministry with Your love, Your peace in all this Lord.
Send forth Your mighty angels to minister to them
personally. I thank You that You are never changing,
true to Your Word, and the keeper of my soul. In
Jesus's mighty name! Amen!

That evening, before I went to bed, I sensed the presence of God in
my bedroom. I was then pressed with these words: "You will be falsely
accused. Stand firm and know that I am with You."

Receiving this, I cried out to the Lord, "Surround me with Your
angels for strength and protection. The joy of the Lord is my strength.
May You forever be glorified in every step I take."

I told Montana that I would be falsely accused, and she
immediately went into prayer and began rebuking it in the name of
Jesus. She could have prayed for hours on this, but in my heart, I knew
it would happen. He said it would—so it would be.

Ye are of God, little children, and have overcome
them: because greater is he that is in you, than he
that is in the world. (1 John 4:4)

And who is he that will harm you, if ye be followers
of that which is good? But and if ye suffer for
righteousness' sake, happy are ye: and be not afraid of
their terror, neither be troubled; But sanctify the Lord
God in your hearts: and be ready always to give an
answer to every man that asketh you a reason of the
hope is in you with meekness and fear: Having a good
conscience; that, whereas they speak evil of you, as of
evildoers, they may be ashamed that falsely accuse
your good conversation in Christ. (1 Peter 3:13–16)

CHAPTER 15

# My Last Day

———

**B**efore the end of summer, I was released from the ministry. I had left the departure letter the night before, which they found, and Sarah sat me down to talk about it.

Her very first remarks toward me were that she loved me dearly. I did not argue with her about that. I believed her. I loved them both dearly. As she continued, I listened to all she had to say.

She shared with me that if she left Sam, she would have nowhere to go—and no money to support herself. She couldn't leave him. We had a heart-to-heart that day, and I respected her choices. I had anticipated defensiveness—and perhaps pleas for grace—from the very beginning, but the total opposite had occurred. *She tried to justify his actions.* Sarah knew the truth. It was only a matter of time before it would surface. She thanked me for the work I did and only asked that I turn over all the passwords.

I kept nothing from the office. I turned it all over to her.

She sat at the computer with her head low.

My heart was saddened. As I finished all she had requested and was about to walk out for the very last time, I turned to her and said, "The Lord wants to restore your ministry."

As these words departed my mouth, she bowed her head in sadness. As tears began to build up, I took one last look at her and closed the door behind me.

My parents just happened to be traveling to visit me the weekend I packed and left. I told them this was my last day at the ministry. The Lord provided my family to help me pack. I needed all the help I could get. I needed a moving truck, first and foremost.

We drove into the major town to look for a U-Haul. When I arrived, there were none available in the lot that would accommodate everything I had. I quietly asked the Lord, "What do I do?" As we turned to exit the building, the Lord brought the U-Haul. The exact-sized truck I needed pulled into the lot. I looked at the agent and asked if I could have that one. She said yes. The Lord provided for my needs. Praise God!

As we packed, I thought about telling Grace all that had happened, but a voice clearly said, "She will not believe you." So, I refrained from telling her anything. I began praying and interceding for her before she even arrived at the ministry. I knew she would become my replacement. I had reached out to her in the spring with a simple introduction. We didn't say much; we just said a little about who we were and how we arrived where we were in Christ Jesus.

My family and I spent the weekend packing. By the next day, I was ready to depart. Before I left for the last time, I made sure to let

Hanna know that when Grace arrived and the truth was revealed to her by God, I would like her to contact me. I would help her in any way I could.

I had completed the assignment God gave me. The Lord wanted to restore the ministry. All the error in that ministry needed to be rooted out, destroyed, and thrown down. Only then could it be rebuilt. I was prepared to restore and rebuild. The Lord had shown me that the entire tree needed to be rooted out—all the way to its roots. He was willing, and so was I!

CHAPTER 16

# Never Easy

———

After I retired, I never expected any of that to happen. I was expecting a solid ministry, blooming in the things of the Lord. I just wanted to fall into place and do my part for Him, but the Lord had other plans. Acts 13:22 says, "…I have found David the son of Jesse, a man after mine own heart, which shall fulfil all my will." Think with me a minute on this verse. How was David a man after God's heart? The answer is quite simple. David did all that the Lord said. Despite his imperfections. He wasn't perfect in any way. None of us are. The journey to know more of His heart had begun. He said He would show me more of His heart, and He did just that. The Lord's heart is repentance. There is something greater coming, the greatest revival anyone has ever seen, and the church must be ready.

Are we ready for the masses of people to enter through the church's double doors?

It was not His desire that the ministry was in the condition it was in. He told me He wanted to restore it. We are never too old to learn. That experience was the Refiner's fire.

Looking back on my military career, His hand was all over my life. Every bit of comfort was removed from my life—from living conditions, food limitations, good and bad leadership, separation from loved ones due to deployments, sacrificed time, and money. The list could go on and on. Those who have served in the military understand the minimalist life of sacrifice required. There were many times I could have been killed while deployed to the Middle East. Even then, He knew His perfect plans for my life. I'm not there yet.

During those times in the service, being led by those leaders, I grew the most. Not even knowing the Lord then, He was teaching me through their silence and unhealthy motives. I know now exactly what I want to be and what I don't want to be. I know how to lead.

> He that handleth a matter wisely shall find good: and
> whoso trusteth in the Lord, happy is he. (Proverbs 16:20)

He knew I would obey and not react as most people would have. In my walk with the Lord, when I go through challenging times that test my faith, I humble myself before Him and seek His face for direction. When we remain humble, we remain teachable. There are blessings associated with listening and learning.

> Commit thy works unto the Lord, and thy thoughts
> shall be established. (Proverbs 16:3)

When we can get to the point where we understand His perfect will, perfect plan, and perfect purpose for our lives, we live a life that is established, heart and soul.

I encourage you to take this time to evaluate your life. When challenging times came, I welcomed them with open arms. I want my Lord and Savior to be the center of all things in my life. Prosperity came when I included Him in my decisions.

Depending on your circumstance, ask yourself:

- Are you refining me, Lord?
- Are you trying to teach me?
- Is there a sinful nature I must confront and deal with?
- Am I suffering for righteousness's sake?
- How will this glorify You, Lord?

There isn't a day that goes by that He is not aware of the details of our lives. When challenges rise in our lives, God doesn't need to know what's in our hearts. He already knows. When those circumstances surface, it's for us to see what's in our hearts. He knows every thought, every move, and every motive in our hearts. I encourage you today to pursue holiness and seek His righteousness in your life.

It had been prophesied to me back in 2014 that I would reach leaders. The word was simple, and I didn't know how this would be accomplished—but I know He would make the way. Before I was promoted into the senior ranks of the military, months before I knew I had made rank, the Lord asked if I knew what it meant to be a great leader. In my limited thinking, I knew when the Lord asks a question, I probably need some correction—or He is about to teach me something amazing. So, I replied no and asked Him to tell me. I was expecting a deep revelation from Him that maybe the world didn't even understand.

Instead, His reply was simple. He indicated that I must genuinely love those I am leading. I knew this lesson was given in love, to encourage, comfort, correct, and discipline—just like a mother and father do when they raise their children. They raise their children to be strong in the Lord, effective individuals who are able to stand on their own two feet when they depart to live on their own.

I cared for Sarah and Sam. I love them dearly, but I know it was the Lord's heart for repentance. He knew what I needed to push through that difficult time. It wasn't easy. It was like a crash course in discerning His voice, receiving interpretations, refining my prayer life, persevering, not harming His anointed, knowing their fruits, discerning good and evil—in character and behavior—fulfilling His will, knowing when to leave, interceding, engaging in spiritual warfare, not gossiping, not complaining, not murmuring, walking in His nature, and obeying.

It was about His grace, His favor, faith, peace, joy, mercy, compassion, leadership, everlasting purpose, repentance, seeing the good through the bad, guarding the heart, discerning when to speak and when *not* to speak, protecting the sheep, seeking His face, pursuing righteousness, healing, deliverance, excellence, the fear of the Lord, mixing spirits, deception, and, most importantly, love. God is mercy and compassion.

> For he shall have judgment without mercy, that hath shewed no mercy; and mercy rejoiceth against judgment. (James 2:13)

If it had not been for that one spoken word from the Lord, I would have never grown spiritually: "I will bless your military career; you will go all the way. But if you choose the ministry, I will show you more of My heart." David was a man after the Lord's heart. Despite

David's imperfections in his life, he obeyed all that the Lord said. Learning to hear His voice is key to pursuing the Heart of the Father.

The Lord desires repentance. The Lord's heart is patient and kind. His heart does not envy or boast. He is not proud, nor does He seek to dishonor others. His heart is not self-seeking, not easily angered. In fact, He keeps no record of wrong-doing not delighting in evil but in Truth. His love always protects, always trust, always hopes, and always perseveres. He will never fail you in His love. Let love be our greatest gift.

Father, show us Your heart for we dearly delight in Your ways. No matter what the circumstance was, is, or is going to be, let Your love manifest in our words and actions, even if I look like the fool, or the enemy. I don't care as long as You are with me, I can do all things through You. Help me be more like Your Son Jesus, who was, is, and always will be LOVE. I need Your love. I need Your heart. Whatever You are doing in me, I will allow you to do it. You are the Potter and I am the clay. Let love be my greatest gift, Father. Teach me through Your word, teach me to hear Your voice. I will obey all that You say. In Jesus name, AMEN!

# About the Author

Virginia Hall was born in Texas. After graduating High School in 1996, she enlisted into the Air Force. Her commitment to service, placing service before self, she served in various countries such as Korea, Iraq, and Afghanistan just to name a few in which she was pulled out of her comfort zones each time. In 2013, during her deployment to Leatherneck, Afghanistan, she was born-again then filled with the Holy Spirit. This life changing encounter altered the course of her life wholeheartedly in which she devoted her life fully to the Lord Jesus Christ. She is now retired and more on fire for the Lord than ever before.

Printed in the United States
by Baker & Taylor Publisher Services